The 10 Most Common Signs of Possession

1. Low energy level
2. Character shifts or mood swings
3. Inner voice(s) speaking to you
4. Abuse of drugs (including alcohol)
5. Impulsive behavior
6. Memory problems
7. Poor concentration
8. Sudden onset of anxiety or depression
9. Sudden onset of physical problems with no obvious cause
10. Emotional and/or physical reactions to reading *The Unquiet Dead*

Also by Edith Fiore
Published by Ballantine Books:

YOU HAVE BEEN HERE BEFORE:
A Psychologist Looks at Past Lives

THE UNQUIET DEAD

A PSYCHOLOGIST TREATS SPIRIT POSSESSION

Edith Fiore, Ph.D.

BALLANTINE BOOKS • NEW YORK

 Published in the United States by Ballantine Books, a division of Random House, Inc., New York, and simultaneously in Canada by Random House of Canada Limited, Toronto.

Library of Congress Catalog Card Number: 86-29096

ISBN 0-345-35083-9

This edition published by arrangement with Doubleday & Company, Inc.

Manufactured in the United States of America

First Ballantine Books Edition: September 1988

This book is dedicated to the seven most important women in my life

Edith Holbert, my mother

Gail Nava, my oldest daughter

Dana Plays, my middle daughter

Leslie Strong, my youngest daughter

Cynthia Nava, my granddaughter

Madeleine Fiore, my stepmother

Ilah LeMoss, my mother-in-law

This book is not meant to be a substitute for medical or psychological help. I always recommend that my patients see a qualified physician for their physical problems. If you have emotional or mental problems, you should seek the help of a professional therapist or counselor.

* Contents

	Foreword	ix
	Preface	xi
1	*An Introduction to Possession*	1
2	From the Natural to the Supernatural	5
3	Historical Observations of Spirit Possession	13
4	What Happens When You Die	21
5	Why Spirits Remain Among Us	28
6	The Effects of Possession	34
7	Case Study—Tony	45
8	Case Study—Anne	53
9	Case Study—Peter	65
10	Case Study—Barbara	79
11	Case Study—Paolo	90
12	Spirit Entry	109
13	Detecting Spirit Possession	119
14	How to Do a Depossession	124
15	Protecting Yourself from Entities	137
16	Detecting, Releasing, and Protecting Your Home from Spirits	142
17	Some Further Thoughts on the Unquiet Dead	153
18	Questions and Answers	158
	Glossary	164
	Bibliography	170

* Foreword

by Raymond A. Moody, Jr., M.D.,
author of LIFE AFTER LIFE and THE LIGHT BEYOND

Is it possible that a disembodied "spirit" or "entity" from the "beyond" can seize control of the mind of a living human being in such a way as to cause that person distress in the form of disturbances of consciousness and of behavior? Despite the fact that Western psychology and medicine by and large have dismissed this possibility as unworthy of serious consideration, human beings from many cultures, and over a period of thousands of years, have insisted that it is a reality. Furthermore, in these cultures various methods of "depossession" or "exorcism" have been employed for alleged possession illnesses, often with apparent healing effect on the sufferers.

Frankly, I have no idea whether "possession" is ultimately "real" or not, but I do know two things. First, that I—like many other psychiatrists—have encountered in my practice a small number of very troubling cases in which the person involved seemed to be suffering from some peculiar alteration in consciousness which did not seem to fit within any category of mental illness known to me, and yet which resembled the description of "possession" found in medieval literature. Secondly, it is fairly clear that persons who are treated as though they were suffering from a "possessing entity" sometimes report dramatic resolution of their symptons after these procedures. Obviously, neither of these facts necessarily implies that possession is "real" in a factual sense, but together they do suggest that we may be dealing here with an unusual variety of human consciousness which is distinct from mental illness and which is worth investigating in its own right.

Oddly, since the early part of the twentieth century, it has been unfashionable among professionals in the field of psychology to explore, in a careful and introspective way, the many unusual and sometimes spectacular alterations to which human consciousness is prone. In this climate, the early pioneering work of such scholars as William James has been rejected and treated with contempt by persons who seriously stated that the study of mind as awareness is impossible, and that the only thing which can be studied under the rubric of "psychology" is "objectively observable behavior."

Presently, we are seeing a change in this attitude, and today a large number of serious, well-trained professionals in the field of psychology and medicine are actively engaged in the study of altered states of awareness. My colleague and friend, Dr. Edith Fiore has made a most interesting study of one of the most controversial of these states—the ancient enigma of possession. Whether or not, like me, you have questions about the ultimate "reality" of possession, no doubt you will be fascinated by this vivid and engaging account of her explorations on the frontiers of the human mind and spirit.

✲ Preface

In *The Unquiet Dead,* I am not attempting to prove that spirits exist nor that my patients were possessed. Rather, I will be showing you what goes on daily in my office and introducing a therapy that, although not a panacea, is effective and embodies ancient concepts within the context of twentieth-century hypnotherapy.

My patients and I use the working hypothesis that personality *does* survive the death of the body. Through the years, many people have reported to me that they have experienced the spirits of their loved ones, sometimes immediately following their deaths. Often it was just a *knowing* that they were there. At other times, they were seen or heard, or an identifying odor was noticed: their perfume or favorite pipe tobacco, etc. These spirits were not earthbound, but came to say "good-bye" or were "visitors" from the spirit world there to give comfort or help. The entities that had not made successful transitions to the afterlife were the ones that caused problems by affecting people in harmful and destructive ways through possession.

Helping these possessing spirits to leave resulted in eliminating their devastating effects, often dramatically changing lives. Because depossession works, I felt a need to write this book. What you will be reading may disturb you, but I hope it will help you by explaining what you have been experiencing in yourself or with others. It will offer hope that problems that up to now have seemed insoluble can be resolved, and that techniques for achieving this goal can be found. At the very least, you may gain a new perspective for understanding human behavior.

What will be revealed also invites you to open your mind to the possibility that life *does* continue after death—and this belief itself can have a profound and far-reaching effect on you.

I am sharing my therapeutic techniques for both nonprofessionals and therapists who would like to include them in their armamentarium. In a sense, certain chapters could be viewed as a training manual for professional healers.

The case material that has been used in *The Unquiet Dead* is of such a personal and sensitive nature that it was important and necessary to protect my patients' privacy. For this reason, I have obscured only their identities, while retaining the essential qualities that they presented.

Many of the verbatim transcripts that illustrate the case studies, as well as some of the chapters of this book, were repetitious and rambling. Therefore, I have edited them in the interest of clarity and succinctness.

Most of the cases you will be reading about were straightforward and uncomplicated in their solutions. But one involved connections between the two "principals," the patient and the spirit, that went back into a past lifetime. However, you do not need to believe in reincarnation to benefit from the findings or the techniques I shall be describing.

Now, let us examine the role of spirit possession in human lives. Chapter 1 will introduce you to this fascinating and surprising subject.

* Acknowledgments

I wish to express my gratitude to:

My five patients who allowed me to report their case studies;

My patients, whose courage and experiences contributed to an understanding of the unquiet dead, and to my own spiritual growth;

Jeffrey Mishlove, Ph.D., for his thoughtful critique of chapter 3;

Margaret Jane Kephart, for her pertinent contributions to chapter 3;

Ormond McGill, for his friendship, perceptions and encouragement;

Ted Chichak, for his enthusiasm for my work which supersedes his responsibilities as my literary agent;

Jim Fitzgerald, for making this book a reality as my editor;

Emma Darknell, for her patience, skill, friendship and interest as my typist;

Jon Kennedy, for his expertise as my writing teacher and for editing the manuscript;

Chris Carney, Harriet Handler, Kathy Iverson, Barbara Jones and Barbara Shipley, for their helpful critiques;

Reginald Fitz, for the title of this book and his contribution to the manuscript.

1 * An Introduction to Possession

> The nurse said "DOA." I was above my body in the Emergency Room looking down. It was too gory, I didn't want it to be saved . . . a bad accident. I heard this terrified scream for help. I thought, Maybe I can help somebody, they can't help me here. I went to help. There was a young boy . . . being operated on. It was the spirit screaming, not the body. The body was on a table, but six feet above that was the boy . . . but he was like me. He was panicky, so I talked to him as a friend . . . and I asked him to talk to me. He finally calmed down . . . and we've been friends ever since.

That encounter took place forty-six years ago. Albert had been with my patient, Howard, every day since—within his body—as a possessing spirit.

Albert came out of hiding after three years of hypnoanalytic therapy. As he put it, "I ain't going to talk to you! I don't need your help."

He surfaced because—on a hunch—I regressed Howard to his tonsillectomy at four to see whether he had picked up an earthbound entity. Certain clues had pointed in that direction.

I was interrupted rudely during my hypnotic induction by an angry, unfamiliar guttural voice issuing from Howard. "He don't need your help!" With that pronouncement, I began an intensive therapy with the spirit, who later identified himself as Albert. After three sessions, he appeared to leave reluctantly with two cronies from the spirit world.

Two weeks later, Howard bounded into my office with a huge grin on his face. Before he sat in the reclining chair, he excitedly reported:

> I have no desire to eat! For the first time in my life, I'm totally uninterested in food. Believe it or not, I had a hard time actually finding something that appealed to me. And I didn't even finish it! All this is a new experience. And in the first four days, I lost seven pounds!

Relaxing back a bit in his chair, he continued:

> I really feel encouraged that I will get rid of these last ninety pounds—and once and for all end my battle of the bulge.

Brenda, a tall, stunning black woman in her late twenties, was seeking relief from pains over most of her body that had defied medical specialists for years. Under hypnosis—and regressed to the cause of her pains—she relived her anguish upon learning that Ann, her closest friend's young daughter, had been mangled badly in a near fatal car crash. She spoke with reverence of her deep love and attachment to Ann.

Then she reported going into Ann's hospital room where she was being kept alive on a respirator:

> I want to go in by myself. I walk in . . . I look at her . . . it doesn't look like Ann, doesn't look like her at all . . . so bruised and crushed. Her head is so large—but she is so tiny, so little. The nurse says, "We can't do anything for her." I just look at her. I wish I could do something. (Crying.) She's so pretty—she *was* so pretty, so cute. Something has to be done for her! I don't know what to do. I just look at her . . . I pray . . . I'm so upset! Maybe . . . maybe I can take her to . . . I could keep her alive. I *can* do something for her! I'm in charge. And I'll take care of everything. I'll be the first to see her body . . . I'll shop . . . and dress her up real pretty . . . and I'll arrange the

funeral . . . and get everything for her . . . the coffin . . . the flowers . . . make her look pretty again. (Long pause.) She's with me now . . . she's with me and I like it!

Brenda's body had been twisting and contorting during the regression. I advanced her to the present and—while she was still deeply hypnotized—explained, "Ann needs to be released, Brenda. Her spiritual progress and happiness depend on her going into the spirit world. She's a prisoner here. I'm sure you don't want that for her. Let her go now."

"It will be hard, but I'll do it," she acquiesced, wiping tears from her cheeks. She then said "good-bye" to Ann. Within minutes, the depossession was completed.

Howard and Brenda are two of the more than five hundred possessed patients I have treated during the past seven years. They came to my office suffering the gamut of psychological and psychosomatic symptoms and problems.

Since I became aware of this phenomenon, I've found that at least seventy percent of my patients were possessed and it was this condition that caused their dis-ease. Most of these people were relieved—through depossession techniques—of more than one entity. Occasional patients were unwitting hosts to as many as fifty or more!

Possession is a relative condition. When it is complete—which is rare—the original personality seems to be gone and is replaced by that of the earthbound entity. Usually, there is a vacillating balance between the two; at times, the spirit exerts only slight influence, while at others, he or she can be extremely dominant. In some cases, there is an ongoing inner battle for control, replete with mental dialogues—even insults and commands!

The spirits that possessed my patients were once people from all walks of life, who—after death—remained in the physical world and became "displaced persons." They had not made the proper transition between the earth plane and the "other side" at death. Sometimes years later, without bodies of their own, they merged accidentally or intentionally with people whose lives thereafter were never the same. For these spirits, there was no worse fate than sentencing themselves to residing in other individuals' bodies, for they thereby postponed their chances to enter the spirit world where they belonged.

Another class of spirits, historically called demons or devils, are believed never to have been human beings. There are documented cases of their devastating and, in some instances, fatal effects. The Catholic Church has taken this form of possession very seriously and uses especially experienced priests who—after extensive investigations and preparations—perform a highly structured exorcism, the Roman Ritual. Many exorcists have suffered great injuries physically, mentally and emotionally, or even lost their lives, as a result of these encounters.

Fortunately—to my knowledge—I have never treated a patient who was plagued by demons. Demonic or satanic possession is not within the scope of this book. For those who may wish to pursue the subject, there are relevant references in the bibliography.

Drawing upon my case files, I shall show you how people become vulnerable to entities and what happens when spirits entwine with their personalities.

You may wonder how I, as a clinical psychologist, became involved in this unorthodox psychotherapy.

Chapter 2 will describe my background and how my therapy evolved, changing my view of life.

2 * From the Natural to the Supernatural

The topic on an hour-long broadcast was the difference between a psychoneurotic and a neurotic. I was listening clandestinely to it in my bed late one night at the age of thirteen. It opened up a whole new world—the world of aberrant behavior. I was fascinated! Then and there, at 11 P.M., I decided to become a psychologist and treat people with these disorders.

The distinctions no longer exist, but my interest in abnormal psychology and the workings of the mind has continued unwaveringly to the present. Looking back, I realize that what really intrigued me was the concept of the subconscious mind that was discussed and illustrated by its outcroppings—phobias, obsessions, compulsions, etc. The inner mind, I now believe, is our greatest challenge and just as worthy of research as outer space.

My curiosity is continually whetted by my patients' probes beneath the surface of their conscious minds. With the experience that has come from doing more than twenty thousand hypnotic regressions with over one thousand patients, I often am able to successfully predict (to myself) what we shall find with these explorations. But still each case is like an intricate jigsaw puzzle that we put together by picking up a random piece here and another isolated one there. When the last significant piece is pushed in place, there is an instantaneous cure. Sometimes the process is speedy and smooth. Much of the time it is slow and tedious as hidden facets surface.

* * *

I was brought up on the East Coast in a very comfortable environment with lots of stimulation from my creative and energetic parents. My father, a portrait painter and cartoonist, was a loving, warm person who encouraged me to push my potentials from childhood through our last times together before his death. He gave me the courage to have faith and confidence in myself. Because of his emotional support and interest, I learned to take risks, which allowed me to explore dimensions of therapy that went far beyond my training.

My mother's zest for life, coupled with her strict Germanic approach to child rearing, developed in me an easy self-discipline, love of hard work and persistent optimism. All of these qualities have been invaluable in treating troubled people during the past seventeen years.

After two years of college, I married at twenty and then became a mother. Years later, I completed my studies as an undergraduate, entered graduate school at the University of Maryland, and finally received my doctorate in clinical psychology from the University of Miami in 1969. My education in psychology was strictly along behavioral lines, with a very heavy emphasis on research and a downplay of therapy.

Interestingly, at the college and universities I attended, Freud was hardly acknowledged for his contributions to our understanding of the human mind and human behavior. And I don't remember more than one paragraph's mention of hypnosis in all my college and graduate school texts or classes.

During my early years as a therapist I worked with emotionally disturbed children. After being on the staff at a children's psychiatric clinic, I developed a private practice, working with children, couples and adults. I began to read about new therapeutic approaches, and incorporated some of these techniques and viewpoints into my work.

After moving to California, I attended a self-hypnosis workshop at Esalen Institute and began to include relaxation and hypnotic suggestions in my therapy. Because of my intense interest in the inner motivations behind symptoms, I saw hypnosis as one of the fastest ways to reach the subconscious mind, the repository of all memories. As I felt more comfortable with hypnosis, I started using a hypnoanalytic approach, which I have employed for the past eleven years.

At first my patients found the causes of some of their problems in early childhood events they had totally repressed. Even more traced their symptoms to the birth experience. Often, traumas sustained at birth and things said at the time of delivery had a profound and lasting effect. Amazingly, some of my patients spontaneously retrieved lost memories of the intrauterine period, between conception and birth. One dramatic resolution of a case of depression stemmed from remembering an attempted abortion. My patient's mind, as a developing fetus, registered that she was unlovable and that her very existence was being threatened. Following the regression, her lifelong depression lifted completely.

One afternoon something happened that changed the course of my professional life—although I didn't realize it at the time. One of my patients, suffering from sexual problems, found himself, under hypnosis, as a Catholic priest in the seventeenth century. When we were discussing the regression before he left, he made it clear that he firmly believed in reincarnation.

Since the concept of past lives had never occurred to me as anything but a rather fascinating and archaic Eastern viewpoint, I was intrigued. But all the more so when he arrived for the next session reporting a complete cure! Before I could sort it all out, another patient spontaneously regressed to a "former life," and she too later stated that she was totally free of her symptoms.

The third and decisive case involved a young woman with a snake phobia who suffered nightmares of snakes at least twice a week, from which she would awaken screaming. Because our search under hypnosis revealed that her phobia did not arise from anything she had experienced in her current life, but rather in a previous incarnation—and feeling a little ridiculous—I directed her to a time before her birth.

She was a particularly deep-level and excellent hypnotic subject. Within seconds she was vividly describing an ancient ceremony, probably in Central America, involving native priests dancing in front of a pyramid with poisonous snakes in their mouths. The snakes represented all that was evil and terrifying, and, at one point, when the priests threw them to the ground, she shook violently—then relaxed with a glorious smile, as the priests beheaded them.

Still in hypnosis, but back to the present, she disclaimed "believing all that stuff," and seemed quite agitated. I gave her a posthypnotic suggestion to forget what she had just experienced.

With this case we have both an unbelieving patient and therapist! Yet she too came back the next time elated because she was free of all the fears she had had. With her face lighting up, she told me that she and her husband had gone camping for the first time, and she felt relaxed and had experienced no anxiety whatever. She added, "Best of all, my nightmares are gone! I haven't had one in two weeks now!" And she continued to remain free of her symptoms.

I still did not believe in reincarnation, but saw the value of this form of therapy, which I definitely regarded as fantasy. I started employing it more frequently until it eventually became a technique I used regularly with excellent results. My book *You Have Been Here Before: A Psychologist Looks at Past Lives* goes into this in depth.

In the early years, I found many patients slipping into other personalities while in the hypnotic trance. I assumed these were multiple personalities and dealt with them as though they were. It did seem peculiar that some patients would have so many "personalities," some who just flitted through. I remember one such "person" who started speaking in a very childish voice and identified herself as "Susie," and asked me if I wanted to play jump rope with her! I never heard from her again.

It was difficult for me to understand what was going on with these patients and especially to fit it into an acceptable theoretical frame of reference. None of these patients seemed to benefit from the investigation of these "personalities," except to feel more comfortable with the various aspects of their personalities that were, at times, making a mess of their lives.

Instead of feeling that they were acting out of character, they began to accept it as another part of themselves. They came to grips a little better with some of their strange behavior. But there was very little change in that behavior!

As I became more interested in metaphysics, because of my experience with past-life therapy, I collected a vast library. Many of the books, including *The Tibetan Book of the Dead,* pictured the typical death experience as very beautiful, with the spirit joining the Light and leaving the body behind. The Light, also referred to as White Light and Bright Light, appeared to represent the god-presence. Some books described cases where spirits—or discarnates—stayed earthbound and often "joined" living people who were unaware of their presence. They then continued to exist on the physical plane by living through these people—often bringing great misery and, at times, even death!

As I read these cases, I reflected back to my earlier work with patients whom I assumed had multiple personalities and wondered whether I had been dealing with spirits. Perhaps entities had been speaking through my patients who were unwilling "mediums." This concept—possession—also explained why some regressions seemed to overlap chronologically. Maybe they were not the patients' past lives but either those of spirits or, if recent, the entities' last lives.

Armed with this new outlook, I began listening carefully when my patients described their problems and behaviors, to detect whether someone else could be causing their suffering.

Many of my patients actually complained of having someone else inside. "My husband says I'm two completely different people, especially before my period" was a frequent comment. Equally frequent was "That's just not me!"

Others confided that "somebody" inside them undermined their resolve to diet, or to stop smoking or drinking, etc. "Somebody says to me, 'You're not going to stick to the diet. By noon you'll be eating again.' " These patients spoke of their conflicts very openly, because they assumed they were talking about two different parts of their personalities—that they were at war within themselves. But I began hearing and interpreting these remarks as possible clues of possession.

Often using finger signals as a guide, I asked the hypnotized patient if a spirit were present. Many times, the "yes" finger lifted. Sometimes, after a revealing hesitation, the "no" finger would lift, but if I then asked whether someone did not want me to know of his or her presence, the "yes" finger revealed the "culprit." I learned also that spirits could manipulate the finger signals in attempts to mislead me!

Taking a quantum leap, I performed depossessions—freeing the "lost souls"—and was surprised when these patients later reported an immediate cessation of their symptoms—some of many years' duration. Particularly sensitive people often described seeing these entities and even their loved ones who were there to take them to the spirit world. Sometimes tears streamed down my patients' faces as they resonated to emotions of the possessing spirits. They could feel overwhelming fear as spirits thought they were being cast out, and joy and relief when they saw their spirit relatives coming for them. Many told of feeling "something leave"—lifting up out of them. Some remarked, "It's less crowded now," "I feel a bit empty," "A big weight's been released," "Now it's possible to be me. I didn't know I was me all these years—that there was a me that could be free."

Again, I found myself in the same position I had been in several years earlier with my first cases of spontaneous regressions to past lives: a nonbeliever participating in something that seemed to work miracles!

During this period I was reminded of an article I had read in the Baltimore *Sun* years before during graduate school days. A rather shocking story was reported of a patient—hopelessly schizophrenic—at one of the most prestigious private mental hospitals in the East. As I remembered it, one Sunday her family dutifully visited her and took her for a drive in the country. *Fortunately*, there was a very serious collision in which she was badly shaken up: Within minutes she was completely sane—for the first time in years—and apparenty remained so!

Putting this together with what was going on in my office, I began to speculate that maybe she had been possessed, leading to a diagnosis of insanity—and later the spirit was forcibly catapulted out of her jarred body.

I wondered if the reason that electroshock therapy sometimes worked very successfully with severely depressed patients was not the same process: the possessing spirit was shocked out of the body of the patient. It seemed to fit with the growing field of knowledge about our bodies emitting an electromagnetic force field. The relapses that had been reported may have been caused by the spirit not going into the spirit world but remaining earthbound and in the vicinity of his former host, the patient. Then, when the vibrations of the patient returned to normal, the spirit could gain reentry.

While I was trying to understand these things, I read in a daily newspaper the remarkable account of an Italian woman who awoke from surgery speaking a foreign language that none of her family understood. Furthermore, not only did she not recognize anyone, she exhibited a completely different personality! Thinking about this, I theorized that one spirit, the original inhabitant of the body, had left and been replaced by another. To me, these were and are fascinating questions.

My work with possessing spirits has made me face again my own beliefs about life after death and the survival of consciousness. Through the years, I have evolved from a disbelief of—but fascination with—the "supernatural" to intellectually accepting the concepts of reincarnation and the continuation of personality. I still am not totally convinced of these at an emotional level and find myself at times questioning and pondering whether it's all fantasy. However, I must admit to myself that the therapy works! Why? Then I intellectually acknowledge the concepts as within the realm of reality again. And so it goes!

My practice now consists of using hypnosis to get to the cause of the problem, whether it is from a repressed memory of an event in this lifetime, past lives or the presence of one or more possessing entities.

I explain to my patients that I am not trying to prove that spirits exist or are possessing them, but that this technique works. I even add that I am not a total believer myself. We agree to use it as a "working hypothesis."

The majority of my patients are very open-minded, or even convinced that spirits exist and that they are possessed. Sometimes they are much more accepting of the idea than I, as are many people in audiences when I lecture on possession. Often, they volunteer "evidence" from their lives or those of someone they know.

I view the possessing entities as the true patients. They are suffering greatly, perhaps without even realizing it. Virtual prisoners, they are trapped on the earth plane feeling exactly as they did moments before their deaths, which may have occurred decades before. They do not seem to profit from any positive activities or education that their hosts have experienced throughout their lives since the possession. Moreover, they are keeping themselves from being in the spirit world which would offer them a beautiful life and afford them the opportunity to make spiritual progress.

My therapeutic goal is to help the possessing spirits, since they are in the greatest pain, even if it means that my patients must be burdened a little longer while we work on the willingness of the possessors to leave. If I were able to "kick them out," I would be creating a monstrous problem, because they would be, again, displaced persons and perhaps latch onto other unsuspecting people who may not seek help. This could possibly lead to suicides or murders at the very most, and misery for the possessed at the least.

Depossession can be immediately and lastingly effective in bringing about complete relief of symptoms. It is an easy technique to use in uncomplicated cases. Fortunately, it does not require mental health training as hypnoanalysis (regression) does.

Sometimes, however, it can be very painstaking with stubborn entities who dig in their heels and refuse to go. In chapter 14 I shall share with you my thoughts about how you can do a depossession on yourself and others, and I shall include verbatim transcripts of the actual depossessions I use with my patients.

Now, let's look back through history to see the various viewpoints on possession and its resolution.

3 * Historical Observations of Spirit Possession

In the last quarter of the twentieth century, many may consider it superstitious to believe that spirits of the dead are a cause of misery and suffering among the living. This is particularly true now, since most scientists are committed to finding biological causes for nearly all human disease, mental as well as physical. However, a brief glance at the literature reveals that throughout history people frequently have attributed the roots of much illness to possessing spirits and many different rituals have been used to exorcise them.

Jesus himself was reported to have cast out spirits on many occasions.

> Jesus preached and cast out devils *(Mark 1:39)*.

> A certain man which had devils a long time . . . Jesus had commanded the unclean spirit to come out of the man . . . He that was possessed of the devils was healed *(Luke 8:27–33)*.

> Master, I have brought unto thee my son, which hath a dumb spirit . . . And he asked his father, How long is it ago since this came unto him? And he said, Of a child . . . Jesus rebuked the foul spirit, saying unto him, Thou dumb and deaf spirit, I charge thee, come out of him, and enter no more into him. And the spirit cried, and rent him sore,

> and came out of him: and he was as one dead; insomuch that many said, He is dead. But Jesus took him by the hand, and lifted him up; and he arose *(Mark 9:17–27)*.

These are only three examples of the more than twenty-six I found in the Bible of Jesus exorcising spirits.

During the early Christian period, the ability to cast out spirits was viewed as a sign of true discipleship.

> Jesus gave his twelve disciples power against unclean spirits, to cast them out *(Matthew 10:1)*.

Even before the birth of Christianity, the ancient Greeks and Romans held well-established beliefs about the so-called dead and their effects on people.

> A sick man pining away is one upon whom an evil spirit has gazed. *(Homer)*

> Certain tyrannical demons require for their enjoyment some soul still incarnate; being unable to satisfy their passions in any other way, incite to sedition, lust, wars of conquest, and thus get what they lust for. *(Plutarch)*

> Demons are the spirits of wicked men. *(Josephus)*

There have always been various viewpoints regarding the nature of possessing spirits. In some cases, people believed that they were actually the deceased. In other instances, they speculated that some spirits had never been in human form, but were instead servants of Satan, or even Satan himself. In this chapter, we shall be examining the former.

Certain cultures had very definite ideas about where possessing spirits originated, and why they interfered with people's lives. The Chinese have had a tradition of ancestor worship that goes back more than ten thousand years. In their view, a person goes through many cycles, or lifetimes. One must stay on good terms with one's ancestors, because they continue to exist in another world—and, if angered or upset, can return to exert harm in this one.

The Japanese, too, have practiced ancestor worship and believed in earthbound spirits. Perhaps this explains the popularity of the rapidly growing exorcistic cult Mahikari, which had four hundred thousand members throughout the world in 1970. Known as the True-Light Supra-Religion, it holds that possessing spirits cause more than eighty percent of human ailments—physical as well as emotional. Their exorcisms are claimed to be able to restore the possessed person to health and well-being, and thousands are treated daily by these techniques.

The ancient Egyptians also believed that the living were affected by the dead, especially the spirits of people who were mistreated or dishonored after death. The ancient tombs are testimonies to their elaborate belief-system that life continues after death. Bodies were mummified so that they could be used again; the inner organs carefully preserved with herbs and concoctions in burial jars for the same purpose. The tombs were repositories of household articles, food, seeds, animals, and servants to continue their way of life. Even wives were sealed alive in the tombs to accompany the deceased on their journeys in the underworld.

Several of my patients—during hypnotic regressions—have traced current problems, such as claustrophobia and fear of the dark, to being buried alive in these tombs. They remembered their terror as they watched the torches diminish and experienced their breathing becoming more strained before their deaths from suffocation.

One of the most highly developed philosophies of the spirit world and its relation to living people comes from Asia. The ancient religion of India—based on the Vedas, which are holy scriptures—was the forerunner of modern Hinduism and Buddhism, which millions still practice today.

Indian scholars perceived humans as having at least seven different "bodies" or "vehicles," only the lowest of which is physical. The rest are nonphysical and invisible to ordinary human sight. These bodies correspond to different planes or levels of reality, and each is finer—vibrating at a higher frequency—than the ones below it.

The body nearest to the physical is known as the etheric, and is the most dense—in terms of its vibrations—of the invisible bodies. On occasion, it can be seen by those with psychic sight—clairvoyants. It is shaped exactly like the physical body, and actually is a duplicate of it. Interpenetrating with the physical body, it controls its health and extends a few inches beyond it.

The next higher vehicle is the astral or emotional body, which interpenetrates both the physical and etheric bodies, extending several inches beyond them, forming an oval of colored lights. Since it controls the emotional aspects of human beings, it is perceived as constantly changing, resonating to the emotions of the person.

The mental body is even finer in its vibrations than the astral. It also interpenetrates the others, and contributes to the expanded aura.

An even more refined vehicle is the spiritual body. Residing outside of the individual on the spiritual plane, it is nonetheless part of our being.

Esoteric teachings discuss still higher bodies, like the causal (one of the fastest-vibrating spiritual vehicles).

The Indian theory, based on the writings of ancient scholars, is that there is an entire world, the astral plane, that exists between the physical and the highest spiritual worlds. It is not a place, but rather an incalculable number of planes, subplanes, and divisions of subplanes, which rise in a gradually ascending scale, as a result of the increasing frequency of vibratory rate.

The lower astral plane is the world of earthbound spirits. In the higher planes of the astral world reside the spiritually evolved entities that are known as guides, masters or teachers.

It is believed that living human beings often "travel" in their astral bodies to the astral plane during sleep, in certain trance states, and deliberately, by willing a part of themselves to leave the physical body. The latter is referred to as "astral projection" or "out-of-body experiences."

The Vedas describe death as the sloughing off of the physical body. The individual continues, journeying into higher planes of existence, bringing along memories. After a stay in the astral world, the soul continues to rise to the mental plane, again leaving behind a corpse—the astral shell. Later, the individual goes to a still higher level of the astral plane, awaiting rebirth in a physical body.

This recycling of the true essence of a person from one physical body to another and the doctrine of karma—the law of cause and effect—are essential for spiritual evolution, according to the Vedic system. It is through reincarnation that individuals can purify themselves in order to enter the highest plane, and rejoin the godhead.

But these all-important cycles can be blocked if people are still obsessed with earthly desires at the time of their deaths. In this case, they remain in and are trapped by the vibrations of the physical plane. Seen as in the lower astral level, they are as close to the earth plane as possible, futilely attempting to satisfy their addictions and desires. While in this lowly state, these earthbound entities cannot make any spiritual progress. They cannot be released from their lower vehicles and rise to higher states.

Often, according to Vedic theory, ignorant or malicious discarnates seek out living people to possess, in order to continue their earthly life. They are able to gain access because the astral body, visible to them in the person's aura, has some defect through which they enter. After they have incorporated, they exert their control, which is always of a negative nature.

This view of possession has been passed down in India and Tibet and is now part of the famous Tibetan medical tradition, which is practiced by the expatriate Tibetans in northern India.

Some of the tenets of the ancient Vedic tradition resurfaced in the West during the nineteenth century in two movements, Theosophy and Spiritualism. Although they held many conflicting beliefs, both of these viewpoints strongly held to the belief in the continuation of the individual personality after death.

Since our search has to do with possession by earthbound spirits, of particular interest is the influence of these two movements on healers in various parts of the world.

Spiritualism had a profound and catalytic effect on South American mysticism through the books of the French writer Alan Kardec. Kardec wrote on the immortality of the soul and the nature of spirits and their relationships with men. He claimed his books were dictated to him by spirits of a higher degree, transmitted through mediums.

Today the influence of Spiritualism has led to rituals of depossession used by healers, mediums and even some modern medical doctors and psychologists in South America.

While lecturing at the First International Congress on Alternative Therapies in São Paulo in 1985, I was given a tour of the Federation of Spiritism of São Paulo, which is an organization housed in a large school-like building. Thirty-five hundred mediums, coming from all walks of life—from illiterate servants to lawyers—treat fifteen thousand patients per week—without a fee! Since the mediums believe they are being used by healers from the spirit world, it is an article of faith not to charge. Their work mainly consists of removing spirits by *desobsession* (depossession).

I was told at the Federation that one out of five inhabitants of São Paulo is a medium. There are twelve million people living in São Paulo! São Paulo is no exception; mediumship is rampant in all of Brazil.

In the United States an early Spiritualist psychiatrist, Carl Wickland, M.D., worked for thirty years with severely disturbed patients who he felt were possessed by earthbound entities. His wife, Anna—a trance medium—allowed the possessing spirits to speak through her vocal apparatus. Dr. Wickland then conversed with them—in a two-way exchange—and convinced them of their condition. After educating them about the life waiting for them, he persuaded them to leave. With some recalcitrant spirits he would have to resort to using a type of electroshock therapy to forcibly drive them out of his patients. He believed that a group of helpful spirits—the Mercy Band—assisted him in removing the entities, and later oriented them in the afterworld.

His book *Thirty Years Among the Dead,* first published in 1924, is a classic in the field of depossession therapy. In it he outlined his theory of mental illness by spirit possession, and included lengthy transcripts of the counseling sessions he had with the spirits who spoke through his wife's mediumship. Sir Arthur Conan Doyle, a Spiritualist scholar, had this to say of him and his book: "I have never met anyone who has such a wide experience of invisibles. No one interested in obsession or the curing of insanity by psychic means should miss this book."

Another remarkable man—Edgar Cayce—brought the issue of spirit possession as a cause of disease to the attention of the public. As an uneducated young man reared on a farm in Kentucky, Cayce found that he could enter into a hypnotic trance and answer questions on any topic. From 1900 to his death in 1945, he gave more than fourteen thousand trance "readings." Most were for sick people whom standard medicine had not helped.

Although a Southern Fundamentalist Christian and Bible expert while awake, in trance Cayce channeled past-life and mystical readings that discussed concepts of karma, reincarnation, meditation, the theory of ascending planes, multiple bodies, spirit possession, and much more.

In his discourses on earthbound spirits and spirit possession as a cause of mental illness, Cayce went beyond most writers on this subject, suggesting complicated physical-emotional-mental and spiritual causes for the possession.

The cures he prescribed for possession while in trance included the internal use of gold, special low-voltage electrical devices, chiropractic adjustment to close off entrance to the nervous system, massage, dietary reform, and a number of other naturopathic and spiritual techniques.

More recently, in 1982, a British psychiatrist, Arthur Guirdham, M.D., reported his findings in his book *The Psychic Dimensions of Mental Health*. Basing his conclusions on his work of more than forty years, he believes that every form of severe mental illness can be caused by spirit interference. Deeply committed to healing patients, his techniques are similar to Wickland's. He too uses electroshock therapy to dislodge stubborn possessing spirits.

Adam Crabtree, a practicing therapist and scholar of mesmerism, also works with possessing spirits. In *Multiple Man: Explorations in Possession and Multiple Personality*, he describes his understanding of his patients' conditions in terms of both possession by earthbound spirits as well as multiple aspects of people's own personalities. His techniques are more of the persuasive type, as he does not use electroshock. He also works therapeutically with the possessors.

Another type of healer, the shaman, numbers in the thousands throughout the world. The shamanistic tradition—the medicine and religion of the preliterate world—has a history that can be traced back forty thousand years and is found on all continents. It is perhaps best known in the United States in the persons of the medicine men and women among our own Native American groups. These shamans base most of their power on belief in spirits of many kinds, and use rituals to drive out the negative, possessing types.

Recently, because there is a growing recognition of the value of their form of therapy, these healers have begun training physicians and psychologists in shamanistic healing techniques. An open-minded acceptance of the Native American spirit-healing beliefs has reached even that stronghold of academic skepticism, the American anthropological community. One of the best-known anthropological experts on shamanism, Michael Harner, shocked his colleagues and delighted his students by starting a shamanic healing society. He now travels all over the world teaching shamanistic healing techniques.

There is now a rapidly expanding number of mental health workers who use a variety of depossession techniques. As their work is becoming known, others seek training. Besides the authors discussed above, there are many other excellent therapists who daily are freeing patients from crippling emotional, mental, physical and spiritual problems and symptoms by releasing ignorant lost souls who are the true recipients of the therapy.

We have seen that throughout recorded history—and probably much earlier—people have believed in possession by earthbound entities. This belief has cut across all boundaries—in terms of both time and social structure. Unsophisticated people as well as learned scholars and great philosophers have espoused this viewpoint. That does not prove its validity, of course. Like reincarnation, life after death, the soul, and many other concepts, spirit possession most probably cannot be proven.

For me, as a therapist working with troubled, unhappy people in pain—emotional as well as physical—the issue of proof is not a priority. Results are! Because depossession therapy eliminates pain and suffering—in my view—its continued use is justified.

An understanding of the death process is essential to our continuing search into the motivations behind possession—and also to its solution. The following chapter will show you how patients experienced their deaths and after-death states as recalled under hypnosis.

4* What Happens When You Die

Do you wonder what will happen to you when you die? My clinical findings suggest that life *does* continue after biological death. Hypnotized patients regressed to former lives find themselves just as "alive" immediately following the body's death as before. Memories, personality, perceptions, emotions, thinking continue without a break. Indeed, the immortality of the soul appears to be corroborated by past-life regressions.

Researchers in the "clinical death" or "near-death" experience have reported findings that are basically identical to those of my hypnotized regressed patients. Their material was derived from interviews of hundreds of people who had actually died and later were revived. Since 1975 with Dr. Raymond Moody's book *Life After Life*, the field of clinical- and near-death experiences has grown rapidly, with significant agreement among researchers.

The majority of my patients under hypnosis recalling previous incarnations related death experiences that were remarkably similar.

It appears that death involves a smooth, natural transition to a spirit realm with no loss of consciousness. My patients noticed an immediate feeling of relief from the pains, discomforts or fears they had been experiencing just before they left their bodies. Almost all reported a feeling of lifting up and floating. They could clearly see their bodies below and whatever was happening around them. Often they tried to reassure their families that they were fine and alive. With a wonderful sense of freedom, they continued to rise and were drawn to a bright white light. They were joined by loved ones who had already died and often by a wise and comforting highly evolved spirit or guide. They found themselves in perfect bodies; any defect had been corrected. If they had been blind, they would see perfectly; if deaf, they now had sharp hearing. If their bodies were mangled in car accidents, they were whole and intact. Amazingly, their spirit bodies seemed just as real and solid as their physical bodies once had.

If the regression continued, they reported experiences of a rich, full existence in another world. At one point, with wise counselors, they reviewed the life they had left and saw it all as though watching a film. (People who have nearly drowned or narrowly escaped death often report a similar experience of having had their whole life flash before their eyes.) It was clear to them that the purpose of this review was to enable them to see where they passed key challenges and failed others. Spirit counselors pointed out what they still had to learn to make the necessary spiritual progress. The next incarnation was planned, based on this knowledge.

My patient files are filled with transcripts of regressions that illustrate the typical death experience. The following came from a twenty-six-year-old male patient, Joe, who suffered from depression, chronic bronchitis, and a rather odd allergy—whenever he drank milk or ate nuts, he immediately developed thick mucus in his throat which greatly exacerbated his already persistent cough.

Following instructions to regress to the event responsible for his allergies, he found himself as a young man living in Georgia in the nineteenth century. He described a frustrated and angry childhood during which he gave vent to pent-up rage by picking fights, which he easily won because of his hulking size. While still a teenager, he killed a man and ran away to join the Confederate Army. Further hypnotic suggestions to move directly to the event causing the allergies produced the following:

> I'm leaning against a tree and the drummer boy is pouring curdled milk into my beat-up cup. It has a hole in it so I have to drink it as fast as I can before it all runs out. I'm eating the pecans from the ground . . . we haven't eaten

regular food for weeks. I see a very muddy, slow-moving river next to these trees. The other men are lying in the sun or sitting under the trees eating pecans, and we are all dressed in tattered gray uniforms. I am very tired . . . and I am thinking about deserting. My whole life I have always fought, but now I am fighting people who are willing and able to fight back . . . and I'm afraid. I don't see many guns and the ones I do see aren't loaded . . . no ammunition for weeks now. I realize that the knife I have is the only protection left—the only way I can fight back. I hear sounds of running feet and horses' hooves . . . now screams and bugles . . . we are being ambushed!

We jump up and run, trying to get across the creek. My feet keep getting stuck in the rocks. They come up behind us, firing rifles at us, and we turn and fight, though most of us don't have guns. Two soldiers jump on me and hold me under the water, bending my arms back until it hurts my shoulders. I raise my head up out of the water and a young kid with a look of hate on his face starts hitting me with the butt of his rifle, calling me a river rat.

I'm choking and swallowing water. (Long pause.) Now I have a floating feeling as though I'm rising out of my body, and at the same time I watch my body float down the creek along with other bodies of boys I know. I look around and see that they have also risen from their bodies, and I turn and see my grandfather bathed in golden Light. He says, "Come on, boy, the war is over." Several other boys I know come too; people liked my grandfather in our town. He says to them, "Come on, y'all. The war is over for you too."

I feel a great sense of relief. I hear a piano and other voices too; one very, very clearly. The voice is like a spark, and I almost hear it, but not quite. I'm almost like a spark myself and that's all there is. I can see the world clearly, yet rapidly, as if everything is moving at a very fast speed.

I pick out the things I did wrong. I'm being told of my mistakes and I'm aware of them without feeling bad. I know I've got to overcome anger and hate and learn to be less selfish. I think I made an agreement with the voice in the golden Light.

Most of the death experiences recalled by my hypnotized patients were as uncomplicated and predictable as Joe's. However, occasionally others were quite different. Instead of a smooth transition from one world to the other, some remembered actually fleeing from the Light in terror or turning away from their departed relatives (in spirit) or guides. Many were unaware of their deaths, since they felt alive, and were totally confused and frightened, especially when they could not make any impact on their survivors. These individuals remained earthbound—tied to the physical plane—despite the fact that they had died.

Some of these spirits actually seemed to merge with or possess living people. This process was clearly illustrated in the regression of a young female patient, Linda, who was being treated for a depression so severe that she was imminently suicidal. During the hypnotic work she found herself as one of these "displaced" spirits, a depressed male. The transcript begins a few minutes before his death:

> I feel very depressed. I feel upset and angry and confused. It's about my wife. She's been unfaithful to me. (Crying.) She's beautiful and she's a very happy person . . . and I'm not . . . but she's able to make me feel good. It hurts that she's been unfaithful. I need her! I've been trying hard to be what she wants, but she doesn't love me. (Long pause.)
>
> I see a river that's practically dry and there is a bridge crossing it. (Pause.) Now I'm up on the bridge . . . I don't want to stay here anymore. It's just too painful. Anything would be better than this. There's nothing to keep me here anymore . . . nothing compelling at all. I think I'm losing my mind. (Pause.) I climb up on the railing . . . I jump.
>
> I'm on the riverbed. (Long pause.) I feel very strange . . . my body feels very funny. I can stand up and I can see my body on the sand. But I'm still here! Damn it! It's not fair! I'm so mad . . . it didn't work. It's not fair! I'm very frightened. There is a very bright light around me, very brilliant . . . and I hate it! (Pause.) I want to leave. I'm running down the riverbed away from my body. I'm running into bushes and trees because it's darker now. But something is not right—*something is not right!* I don't understand it. I hit a tree and I go right through it. I'm

> frightened and confused. I don't like this at all! It's like being blind, groping around and hitting things. I'll just lie here for a while . . .

During that same session, the man, now a spirit, went on to recall his attraction to and subsequent possession of a young girl:

> I feel so alone. I've been this way a long time. It's lonely and I'm afraid and angry. It feels like I've been here forever. I hear some people; they're having fun. They are on the beach, playing. I go up to them, but they ignore me. Why can't they help me? Why won't they help me? I'm so miserable and they are so happy. It makes me angry!
>
> There's a beautiful young girl who is happy and lovely—but she won't even stop and look at me—she won't even notice me. (Linda shakes her fists and then looks puzzled.) I tried to hit her; I don't understand; I don't know what happened.
>
> It's like I'm with her now; I'm part of her, somehow. It's much better now. I'm much warmer now. She's very happy and I still feel very sad, but I can feel what she feels. I like it when she feels good. But she's the one having all the fun—and that makes me angry too. (Long pause.) Now she doesn't have as much fun as she used to.

It appears that all spirits eventually go to the Light—even after remaining stuck on the physical plane for decades. With suicides, I have found that many remained as discarnates, feeling just as depressed as they did before their deaths—until they were "rescued" by spirit helpers or they possessed unsuspecting living people. However, others who killed themselves went immediately into the Light.

An interesting description of the journey to the Light was given by a depressed patient who relived committing suicide in a former life. After her death, she lingered on the earth plane for a number of years. When she had recalled these experiences, I advanced her to the time the spirit found the Light.

> It's a long time. I'm confused . . . wandering. I'm trying to raise my level of consciousness. I'm trying, but I can't.

I see memories of Light, but I can't find it. The Light flashes, but it's not here. It appears and disappears. I wander . . . I search. I know the Light means something. When it comes, I feel better. I feel peace from above. I know I have to get nearer to it. I know I *have* to . . . *I have to find it*. I have to get that peace inside of me.

It's coming . . . it's coming. Someone's helping me. Someone's guiding me. Someone's helping me find my peace . . . find myself . . . find my inner being . . . find my destiny . . . my fate.

I'm joining the Light. I'm coming into existence with the Light; but the Light's not the end. The Light's the beginning. There's more to me than the Light. There're spirits beyond the Light. There're more spirits like me.

I'm wandering into the Light. Some spirits go easily. Some spirits go by me so fast! Some are having trouble keeping up with me. I'm trying to find out more about the Light. What's on the other side? What is it that makes these people . . . these spirits go? Why? What is it?

It feels good in here. The coldness is going . . . it's gone. There's heat. There's warmth . . . there's peace, but not total peace. There's more peace and happiness beyond the Light. I can see that. I can feel that. I know it's there. Getting through is not easy, though.

Someone is helping me. I stumble and fall. Oh! My guide is helping me. There're a lot of spirits. I communicate with all these spirits. There's a lot of happiness now. I feel happy. I feel better than I *ever* have. I feel joy. I don't feel alone anymore. I belong to something.

The Light's behind me. It's blue . . . it's crystal blue now. The Light still glows behind me, but everything is blue. It's . . . it's a unity. It's a beginning I never could know. It's a togetherness . . . it's a sharing. I don't know why they are all sharing with me. And I'm beginning to share with them.

I'm leaving my pain. They are making me feel happy. They are giving me strength, eliminating my confusion, guiding me, through their senses—their thoughts—their experience. Now it's over . . . it's over!

From my patients' regressions, it appears that going into the Light is a universal experience. The Light itself is variously described as "God," "unconditional love," "a beautiful light—like the sun," and by most as indescribably beautiful and wonderful. A typical experience of it is "It's warm, and I feel protected. It must be God. I feel forgiveness for everything I've done."

Another frequent description is exemplified by the following:

> I'm not ready to go. No! I want to stay with my friend. My guide said it wouldn't be good for me. I need to bless him and move on. We left. The Light is immense! Just beautiful. And it's warm. All of a sudden, I feel real good. I feel *real* happy! My guide is laughing with me. I'm saying I need to go back to my friend. He's saying it's not possible, that I have things to do. Everything is okay. It doesn't matter what you did or said. It's okay. I feel *so* good!

You have seen how beautiful the death experience is when the individual makes the transition to the Light. Now, it's time to examine the reasons that many resist that experience and remain in the physical world without bodies of their own, and, in their ignorance, condemn themselves to a miserable earthbound existence.

5 * Why Spirits Remain Among Us

From my clinical experience, I have found several basic explanations for why certain entities remain tied to the material plane, rather than completing their transitions to the spiritual world. The most usual are ignorance, confusion, fear (especially of going to hell), obsessive attachments to living persons or places, or addictions to drugs, alcohol, smoking, food or sex. Also a misguided sense of unfinished business often compels spirits to stay in the physical world. Some remain determined to get revenge.

Communicating with these spirits through hypnotized patients, I have learned that some people were so convinced, during their own lifetimes, that there was nothing after death, they simply refused to see the family members or spirit guides who came for them. Instead, they drifted aimlessly in a state of confusion and ignorance that often lasted for years.

When questioned, they usually denied that they were dead at all, saying something like, "When you're dead, you're dead! I'm here now, so I'm no more dead than you are!" If under hypnosis I moved them back to the time of their deaths, and then asked them to look at their own lifeless, physical bodies, they refused to, or claimed that they were asleep or that they belonged to someone else.

In order to convince a particularly stubborn entity that her body had died, I regressed her to the moment of her death. She vehemently stated, "I'm sleeping . . . I'm sleeping on a satin bed. I'm not dead, you know! I'm not! I can't—won't—see any more!" Moments later, she recognized some spirit relatives, including her deceased husband and her close friend. She said, "You're not going to tell me I'm dead. *I'm not dead!* There's Betty. She's dead. She wants me to go to her house. But I can't go with her, because she's dead. Betty's screaming at me, 'You're dead! You're dead!' But, no! I am not dead!" After I spoke to her further about the nature of death, she finally was able to accept her true condition and willingly departed with her husband and Betty.

Some people were in such a profound state of confusion when they died that they simply didn't realize they were dead. This was particularly true of suicides. Many of them, though not all, wandered about without direction, making futile attempts to communicate with the living. This was the case with the person mentioned earlier who killed himself by jumping off a bridge. That spirit could see his body lying in the sand, but the fact of his own death did not make an impression on him. Later, he could not understand why people on the beach did not respond to him.

I have seen cases of suicides where people did experience a normal death process. Regardless, it appears that when they commit suicide, they are only postponing the working out of their lessons and retarding their spiritual progress, for they will have to find themselves in another test situation with suicide as a strong option in some future life.

Confusion was also common among people who experienced a sudden, unexpected death. Some stayed where they died for hours, months—in some cases even years. One young man who was killed in a car accident remained at the scene watching medics put his body into a plastic body bag, without understanding the significance of what was happening. Then—feeling lonely—he drifted to the motel lounge where he had been performing as a musician, and he was shocked when people there couldn't see him and didn't talk to him. In relating this to me, he joked, "I felt like Caspar the friendly ghost!"

Another man who also died in a car crash stayed at the accident site in a daze for over twenty-four hours simply staring at the spot where his car had run off the road into a river, before somehow returning to his home, where he unsuccessfully tried to communicate with his family.

A teenager who was shot in the face couldn't bring himself to leave his disfigured body. He recalled, "I was confused. I didn't know what was happening. I was lost. I didn't know where to go. I remember that the person who shot me just drove away and left me there."

Other entities confessed to being so ashamed of their former deeds that they didn't want to see their spirit loved ones. Often those who were brought up with a strong religious background were terrified of going to hell. These frightened spirits often desperately resisted the helpers who appeared at the time of their deaths.

One refused—on numerous occasions—to go with his mother to the spirit world because he felt horribly remorseful about his earlier practice of devil worship. He believed that she would never forgive him, since she had been a staunch Catholic. The depossession was successful only when his mother finally was able to convince him that she forgave him completely.

Another possessing spirit, a young black war veteran, street criminal and drug addict who had committed suicide, at first refused to leave with his mother and aunt who came for him. "They are good and I can't go where they are, because I did bad things like drink and steal and roll people," he confided.

A young girl who strongly believed hell was her punishment for committing suicide shied away from helping spirits. She finally left when her mother literally dragged her away.

Obsessive attachment to the living was another compelling reason that some entities remained earthbound. Parents stayed to "help" their children as they grew up; marital partners remained out of loving concern for their spouses. But no matter how well-meaning the motives, the attachment of spirits always caused serious problems: the overprotective parents retarded their children's growth and development because they infused them with their fears; the loving spouses became very upset when the widowed survivors remarried and often deliberately created havoc with the new marriages.

In one case, the spirit of a young man stayed near his younger brother who had idolized him in order to "help" him. Because the entity had been a marijuana addict, the living brother began using that drug—and was soon using others as well.

A particularly fascinating case involved a compassionate surgeon who, dying suddenly in a car accident, returned to his own hospital and was drawn to the body of an infant still in the womb and about to be born prematurely. He commented:

> This little soul was to be born so early—seven and one half months and only two and one half pounds—that she needed more. She was too weak to survive by herself. I could give her more; I could give her the strength she needed until she could go on by herself. She was tiny, *so tiny!* She needed me—and I needed her. I still needed to experience things; with her I could experience what I hadn't and wanted to.

After he departed—more than twenty years later—the patient said, "He was kind, but it seems that he had taken over so much that it didn't give me a chance to grow."

Another spirit, a mother whose daughter had died, was reluctant to leave my patient, a seventeen-year-old girl, because the girl reminded her of her own lost daughter.

But motives of possessing entities were not always benign—they often were malicious—even vengeful! Several of my patients were plagued by the spirits of people who had been hostile to them while alive. Many had been besieged by vicious entities whom they never knew. Some actually were harassed by spirits who hated the other spirits already possessing the patients!

A middle-aged female patient was possessed by several entities, among them two sisters. It became clear that the older sister was inhabiting my patient simply because she was following her sister in an obsessive effort to continue controlling her. When the younger sister departed with her loved ones, the entity finally left, much to my patient's relief.

Just as there are individuals whose lives revolve around getting revenge, there are similarly minded spirits. If they had been murdered or felt they had been wronged, they stayed after death to deliberately hurt their "malefactors."

As living people, their vibrations were lower than most and, like criminals and addicts, it was easy for them to remain earthbound. Some were even intent upon killing the person they possessed. You will see an example of this in the cases of Peter and Barbara in chapters 9 and 10.

Spirits also frequently remained tied to the earth plane because they were obsessed with a place, usually their former home or land. In one puzzling case, a female entity possessed my patient as a very young girl, when her family built their house on land that had been the site of the spirit's former home over eighty years earlier. This vengeful entity had first tried to vent her anger on the girl's father and mother. But because the parents' auras were too strong, my patient, then a seven-year-old child, became her victim. From the time of the possession on, the girl's personality drastically changed; she became extremely shy and especially afraid of public speaking.

In her regression, we found that the possessing entity had been publicly hanged as a murderess before a jeering crowd. Her last memory was of "a sea of hostile faces." This miserable spirit had carried the emotions of that traumatic experience into the child she possessed. When she finally left, my patient was immediately relieved of her crippling, long-standing fear and gave a lecture in her church without any anxiety.

One of the strongest ties that bound spirits to the physical world was addiction—to alcohol, drugs, sex, smoking, even food. If a person died while in the grips of such an addiction, the most overwhelming need felt immediately after death was for the addictive substance or sensation. The spirit was blind to leaving, seeking only to fulfill the compulsion. Spirit guides and relatives were ignored; the Bright Light went unnoticed.

I have treated many of these addicted patients. Spirit addicts tended to cluster around living addicts and the places they frequented, attempting to experience again what was once the dominant theme of their lives. They *did* actually experience it again after possessing the individual. From then on, they exercised their control and had what they wanted, when they wanted it!

Almost without exception, when there was a drug or alcohol addiction, the patient harbored more than one entity who also were addicts. A forty-four-year-old female recovered alcoholic, dry for almost four years, but still suffering from deep depression and anxiety, was possessed by eighteen alcoholic entities, some of whom had been with her since she was ten years old!

Patients who were addicted to drugs, including alcohol, usually opened the door to possession by indulging in the drugs first and thus attracted the addicted spirits. But in other cases, they were simply in the wrong place at the wrong time, at a bar or a party that by its nature had already attracted spirits waiting to indulge.

When an important project is not completed, there is often a compulsion to finish it. This can continue after death, frequently tying spirits to the material world. Thwarted in their vain attempts to bring closure to their work, these entities may eventually possess others to live—and work—vicariously through them. Then the possessed feel inexplicable compulsions to do things they had no former interest in.

No matter what needs they are desperately seeking to fulfill, earthbound spirits are immensely frustrated, confused and unhappy; they can find no peace or lasting satisfaction while inhabiting other people's bodies. They are truly *lost souls* who do not know they are hurting themselves.

Their influence on their unknowing hosts' lives and behavior is *always* negative, sometimes fatal! In the next chapter, you will be shown how spirits trapped on the earth plane affect their victims. You will learn about the range of symptoms and problems that are caused by possession.

6 * The Effects of Possession

Earthbound entities, either discarnate or incorporated, seem to remain exactly as they were moments before their deaths. It's as though they have been "freeze-framed"; throughout their stay in the physical world they do not change or profit from anything they experience. They have all their previous attitudes, prejudices, addictions, skills, interests, fears and hang-ups. If their deaths involved physical pain, this continues unabated, even for decades! If they were anesthetized, or drugged by alcohol, prescription or illicit substances before they died, they feel "spacey" and "out of it" for as long as they are earthbound. Possessing entities who committed suicide continue to feel desolate regardless of what their hosts experience. They remain abjectly depressed.

Degree of Possession

The possession itself can range from nearly total, in which case the original inhabitant is almost completely replaced, to a very minor influence. Some of the factors that determine the extent of the possession are the intrinsic strength of the individual compared to that of the possessing spirit, and conditions that weaken the possessee, like stress, drug abuse, illness, etc.

The more the afflicted abdicate control of their consciousness, the greater the influence of their possessors. If the possessed drink, especially if they get drunk, they are unwittingly giving control to the entities. Blackouts are examples of total—though temporary—surrender of the consciousness. That is why others say, "He's a completely different person when he's drunk." He is! His role had been reduced to zero during that time.

Age When Possessed

One of the most important factors in possession is when it occurs. A great many of my patients were possessed as very young children, especially following hospitalizations for such surgeries as tonsillectomies, or during severe illnesses. Picking up a spirit at that tender age and growing up with it "on board" made it nearly impossible for the people possessed to discern the boundaries of their own personalities from those of their possessors. I hear complaints like "I've always had a violent temper" and "My mother told me I had headaches even as a toddler." When the possession occurred in the earliest years, the possessed later is often afraid to have the spirits leave, fearing that "There won't be anything left" or "I won't know who *I* am" or "I'll be lonely!"

The possession weakens the child's aura and creates a vulnerability to further possession. My findings indicate that if people are possessed early in life, by adulthood invariably they are multiply possessed—each entity additionally undermining the integrity and protection of the aura.

On the other hand, if the possession happens when the individuals are older, the "before and after" differences are more clearly differentiated. In these cases, patients make comments like "I've never been the same since the accident" or "I always was a happy child and popular in high school, then, three years ago, I started to withdraw and sank into these black moods." Especially common are remarks like "That's just not me," "I would never do such a thing—but I did," "My husband says I'm like two different people," or "I think I have a multiple personality."

In the majority of cases, there is a blending of the personalities and the onset of the possession is only vaguely perceived, if at all.

Possession by Spirits of the Opposite Sex

When people are possessed by spirits of the opposite sex, their hormonal systems appear to be affected—always negatively.

Some cases of premenstrual syndrome (PMS) often cleared up immediately with a successful depossession. In many patients, one reason for a diminished sex drive was this type of possession.

Possession by spirits of the opposite sex often results in tension and distance between marital or relationship partners. Frequently the possessors dislike the spouses, or even hate them! Since the possessed accept these emotions as being their own, havoc ensues, wrecking relationships. In one of my ongoing cases, a female patient who is severely possessed by an extremely angry young male drug addict became increasingly hostile to her husband. Their relationship deteriorated to the point of separation and ultimately divorce, in spite of my advice to the contrary.

Entities of the opposite sex often are the cause of a great deal of confusion about sexual identity. Homosexuality, transsexuality and transvestism are the extreme results of this kind of possession.

Range or Effects

Physical Symptoms

The very act of possession itself produces fatigue in the individual, sometimes exhaustion. All the possessed patients I have treated noticed a lessening of their energy level. Usually I hear "I'm exhausted by the time I get home from work," "I go to bed at eight-thirty—but I used to be up until 11 P.M." I conceptualize this draining of energy as a result of the possessing spirits having very weak energy systems of their own. They are literally syphoning off their hosts' energy. I explain it to patients as, "It's like one battery taking care of the electrical needs of one and a half cars. The entity doesn't have a body, so he doesn't use as much as you, but his turmoil and thoughts require energy, so he draws off yours."

Spirits seem to bring an imprint of their physical bodies exactly as they were at death. This affects the living organism of the possessees. According to esoteric theory, the spirits' lower astral bodies interact with the etheric bodies of living people, resulting in a blend of the two. This creates a blueprint for the physical bodies and later manifestations of some of the former physical characteristics of the possessors.

Therefore, possession can result in physical symptoms of all kinds, among them: pains, most frequently headaches, including migraines; PMS with edema (water retention); cramping; lack of energy or exhaustion; insomnia; obesity with resultant hypertension; asthma and allergies, etc.

A female patient, Sally, suffered from severe hot flashes that had come on suddenly, even though her menopause had started several years before. She was troubled to the extent of having to change her nightgown and sheets several times every night because of profuse sweating. Even worse, she had to discontinue sleeping with her husband, as he generated too much additional heat. We discovered that she had recently picked up a menopausal spirit who, fortunately, when apprised of her true condition, left without hesitation. Sally was immediately freed of the symptoms, much to her husband's delight!

Another female patient reported that her sciatica, from which she suffered for more than fifteen years, cleared up following a depossession. The identity of the possessing spirit wasn't clarified, so we can only assume he or she was a person who had a sciatic condition.

A chronic neck pain and depression were eliminated completely when the spirit who had hanged himself in prison was taken into the spirit world by his loved ones. My patient felt comfortable, physically and emotionally, for the first time in years.

Some patients complained of feeling "stoned," hung over, or drunk, for no logical reasons. It was only after successful depossessions that they realized who had been responsible—and they were finally freed of these symptoms.

Possession by a spirit who died as an elderly person often results in symptoms that are common with older people, like blurry vision, aches and pains, and general tiredness.

One woman in her twenties had sought medical help for several years for intense abdominal pain and feeling old and decrepit. She was not relieved of these problems until we did a depossession. Her possessor was the former owner of her home, who had died in my patient's—and her—bedroom, of cancer of the intestines at the age of seventy-seven.

As I cautioned earlier, it is imperative if you experience a physical problem to consult your family physician. *Depossession should not be a substitute for good medical care!*

Mental Problems

A great many mental problems result from intervention by spirits. The most prevalent is lack of concentration—"fuzzing out," as one patient put it. Another said, "My mind takes little breaks—like skipping a spot for a while," and "Part shuts off—Blanksville!" Memory problems, like forgetting something done or said, missing exits on the freeway, etc., are typical. In my practice I find occasional "forgetting" of therapy appointments often reflects the spirit's resistance to depossession. This is especially evident when we have been working with recalcitrant entities.

The reason forgetting is a problem is that there are two or even more people inhabiting the same body, all "doing their own thing" from time to time. The possessing spirit may decide he wants ice cream, and the patient "comes to" with her hand on the freezer door and can't remember why she's opening it. This, of course, depends on how the two are interacting. If one takes over and the other phases out, then that kind of behavior is experienced. In other cases, the thoughts of the spirit's mind are picked up and acted upon by the possessed with no break in consciousness.

Some patients remarked that they used to have aptitude in certain areas like math or spelling, and then were hopeless in them. An extreme example of how spirits interfered in mental functioning is the case of Tony, related in chapter 7. You will see how he nearly flunked out of college after a brilliant start.

Emotional Problems

Emotions are always affected when there is possession. Anxiety, fears and phobias were traceable in many cases to the possessors, even though patients initially assume responsibility for the reactions. I often heard such comments as "I always loved driving, but now when I approach the freeway, I go bananas!'' Or ''I've been looking forward to our session all week, but on the way over, I nearly fainted and hardly could restrain myself from walking out of the waiting room! This can't be me!'' A conversation with the fearful spirits revealed who the anxious ones really were.

Phobias frequently are related very logically to the actual circumstances of the former death experience, which the entities vividly remember. When the people they are possessing are in similar situations, all the original fears come back and the possessees, feeling it, assume it's themselves reacting, not realizing they are possessed.

This was the case with a particularly sensitive patient, Lynn, a well-known psychic, who couldn't understand what had happened to her. For seven years, immediately following an elective surgery, she had been unable to drive her car because of feelings of panic. If someone else were driving, she was free of anxiety, unless they drove on the nearby coastal highway, high above the water. This condition was extremely puzzling to her, since one of her former joys in life was racing cars!

Under hypnosis, she easily tuned in to a young female spirit who, suicidal over a broken romance, had impulsively plunged her car off the same highway. She was terrified as she fell to the ocean far below. Her body was taken to the same hospital that Lynn was in. The spirit, disliking the cold of the morgue, and feeling confused and scared, wandered to an upper floor and into Lynn's room, where she soon possessed her.

Even when we had been trying to release a frightened entity from a patient who assumed he was possessed, he still found it difficult to experience the panic and disclaim it as not being his own. The more such a patient could believe it belonged to the entity, the better he could quickly bring it under control.

Depressions often were traced to despondent spirits who usually didn't realize they were dead. As explained in chapter 5, some who committed suicide remained bound to the physical world because they were terrified of going to hell. Many continued to be so depressed that they didn't see their spirit helpers and loved ones. Because they were still suicidal, they posed real threats to the very life of the possessed! Regressions to past lives showed that at times these distraught entities had driven ther hosts to suicide.

Drug and Alcohol Addiction

Next to depression, the most devastating symptom of spirit possession is drug and alcohol abuse. Once addicted spirits gain entrance, they literally have a stranglehold on their victims. Their hosts then interpret the impulse to use drugs as entirely their own. Under the influence of the substance, they abdicate even more control over their lives. This permits the spirits—usually there are multiple possessions—to indulge to their hearts' content. *They* don't have to pay the price in broken relationships, destroyed health, lost jobs and even greater lowering of self-esteem and respect. The aura becomes very weakened from continued drug use, allowing easy possession by still others seeking a puppet, a pushover, or a "sitting duck," as they have been described by their possessors.

Because the original personality is overwhelmed by the addicted spirits, therapy is very difficult—the entities certainly aren't motivated to be helped! In their ignorance, they don't want to give up a "good thing." Fortunately, in exceptional cases I have been able to help some patients become freed from their enslavement—even in one or two sessions! Usually, however, it's a long struggle in which the patient often succumbs and drops out of treatment.

This type of possession can be life-threatening—from a fatal overdose or car accident. Many of my patients have narrowly escaped death, as the following example illustrates.

Glen, a stockbroker in his mid-fifties, sought help because he had suffered from severe insomnia for twenty years. Further conversation revealed a serious drinking problem that had developed suddenly four years before. After a few sessions, we uncovered an alcoholic entity, John, who had possessed him during a hospitalization four years ago. He apparently left with his loved one after an uncomplicated depossession.

A few days later Glen called for an emergency appointment, urgently explaining to my secretary that he couldn't wait for his next scheduled treatment.

As he walked into my office the next day, he looked terrible! After collapsing into the reclining chair, he blurted out, "I slept through the night for the first time in twenty years—the night of our appointment! But when I woke up in the morning, I felt sick!

I could barely make it down to the kitchen to fix my coffee. My head was killing me! I couldn't believe it! There on the counter was the vodka. An entire liter empty! It was unopened the night before. I must have drunk it all. There—next to it—was a whole quart of cottage cheese—eaten, not a spoonful left! I really panicked. It's a wonder I wasn't dead! Thank God, I ate the cottage cheese. And—you know—I don't remember a thing."

Glen continued, telling me that after that he had been confused and extremely depressed. He was terrified of seeing me again and immediately canceled his next appointment. Then he reflected and wondered if John had really left. He picked up the phone and asked to see me as soon as possible.

Under hypnosis, it became clear that John had not gone into the afterlife, but had just left Glen's aura temporarily. As he put it, "I was found out and I felt closed in on." He admitted the depossession had profoundly upset him. It didn't take him long to slip back into Glen's body.

"He was sleeping, but I wasn't. All I wanted was a drink! I was in a panic! I walked down to the kitchen and drank the vodka. Then I thought, I could kill us! So I ate the cottage cheese."

After reassuring John, another depossession was tried. This time I made sure he had a firm grip on his deceased wife's hand and he finally left with her. It worked! Glen lost all desire for vodka from that point on.

Smoking Addiction

Unlike drug abuse, nicotine addiction causes not as much weakening of the aura and no major distortion of consciousness. The effects are less destructive mentally and emotionally, but they take their toll on the individual's health. I've treated people who have complained of incipient emphysema or the threat of lung cancer, who have every reason to stop smoking, but can't. The addicted entities don't care a whit about the health of their hosts. They figure they can find another "patsy" if the host dies. What a relief it is to patients when the depossessions have been successful. They immediately find not only no desire to smoke, but freedom from withdrawal symptoms.

Weight and Obesity Problems

One of the most multidetermined problems that therapists (medical and psychological) deal with daily is overweight or obesity.

Obviously, possession is only one of the many causes of this growing national health concern.

I've had patients who have found entities at the root of their problems with weight control. Not only were the spirits responsible for the weight gain, but they were uninterested in dieting and—in fact—determined *not* to give up their pleasure in eating what they wanted. Sometimes our clues were clear because the weight gain occurred rapidly following a situation in which possession was especially possible: after surgery, the death of a loved one, etc.

Sylvia, a delightful woman in her forties, was overjoyed when her long-term, obsessive craving for sweets—the bane of her chronic weight struggle—left after our first session during which I had performed a generalized depossession. At the beginning of our second meeting, she explained, "I have no interest at all in sweets. I can't believe it! You have no idea how it dominated my life. All I thought of was eating something sweet—and when I did, it didn't satisfy me—I had to exert all the control I could muster up. And I was like that as long as I can remember! Now I don't even think about it!" Spirits bring their cravings with them!

A craving for chocolate left with my patient's deceased father-in-law who had been possessing her since his death. He was known to his family as a "chocoholic"!

Another patient reported that the morning she seriously committed herself to start a diet, a voice in her head said, "I'm not going to let you diet. Forget it! I'm in charge." The possessing entity, which had dominated her for many years, departed only when convinced she could eat all she wanted in the spirit world. The compulsion to overeat vanished with her.

Relationship Problems

Relationships really suffer as a result of possession because there is an unsuspected ménage à trois—or more—involved. An unpleasant child may be harboring a vicious spirit whose values are different from those of the child's family. A husband could be relating to a male spirit possessing his wife. Interplay of the spirits involved between mates or partners often results in erratic sexual attraction. Even employee-employer relationships may be disturbed for the same reason, which is illustrated in the case study of Anne in chapter 8.

Sexual Problems

Since many spirits were old when they died, the people they possessed often experienced symptoms of aging, including a noticeable diminution of their sexual drive.

Sexual hang-ups are part of the repertory many entities bring with them. Their own problems and proclivities manifest themselves when the possessed engage in sex. At one extreme, their hosts may even be prevented from approaching their partners! This was the case with Paolo, whom you will read about in chapter 11.

One of the causes of homosexuality is possession by spirits of the opposite sex. If the possession began before puberty, heterosexual development often was disrupted and the afflicted grew up believing *they* desired sexual partners of the same sex, when it was the entities who were determining their choices. Every homosexual patient I have done a depossession on has had at least one exceedingly dominating entity of the opposite sex who was determining the sexual preference. Often these patients told of feeling they were "trapped" in bodies of the wrong sex.

Some of these people were considering irreversible transsexual operations because of the spirit's desperate attempt to make the possessee's body as much like the deceased one as possible.

I have treated a number of transvestites, *all* with possessing spirits of the opposite sex. It was they who bought the clothes and dressed up to suit their fancy, much to the confusion and embarrassment of their victims.

This chapter gave you an overview of how individuals' lives can be warped by possessing spirits. From the above categories and vignettes, you can see that the effects of possession can be disastrous and, at times, fatal.

The next five chapters—each a complete case study—give an

in-depth view of not only the devastating results of possession, but how it came about originally. You will be shown how depossession therapy benefited these suffering people—the possessed, as well as their possessors.

These cases were picked from my files of hundreds of patients, to give you an understanding of the anguish that ensues from possession, from the people themselves who were—in most cases—the consciously unwilling and unsuspecting victims of spirits.

7 ✻ *Case Study—Tony*

Tony walked hesitantly into my office, his broad shoulders slouching as though he were carrying an overwhelming burden. He sank into the chair, looking exhausted, despite having a youthful, well-muscled body. If he had had a different expression, he would have been the picture of health. Indeed, he was handsome enough to be a movie star. Neatly groomed, thick black curly hair framed an attractive, rugged face that reflected his Italian heritage.

Frowning and groping for the correct way to express his feelings, he began: "My whole life has changed and I'm scared! I used to be an A-student and now I'm actually failing—my grades are equivalent to twenties and thirties! I'm flunking out of college. My whole future is going down the drain! I don't know what's happening."

He explained that for the past four months he had been unable to concentrate and even remember material that he had just read. Far worse, he found it hard to understand his professors, when before he had been fascinated with the subject matter and was at the top of his class. He wanted to be a physician. Now, he was wondering if he'd be doing manual labor all his life.

Dr. Adams, an oncologist and family friend, had been helping Tony decide on a medical specialty. There was a close rapport between the two and, from his description, Dr. Adams sounded like a very unusual physician. He had the ability to see auras and "read" people with precise intuition. He also had strong healing abilities, which he quietly used when he touched people during physical examinations. Tony confided that his friend had expressed great concern about him during this four-month period and had encouraged him to seek my help.

"Tony, there's a solution to every problem. When we see smoke, we know there's a fire somewhere. Our job is to find the fire—and put it out! Can you remember exactly when this problem began?"

"I don't know what caused it. One day I was different! I thought maybe it was the stress of only having a few months left before I graduated and worrying about whether I would be accepted by a medical school. Then, there was all the extra pressure of exams and reports. They all seemed to be due at the same time."

He added that he was having trouble with his girlfriend. "The slightest thing makes me explode! I'm irritable with her most of the time. I don't understand this—we got along beautifully before. Sure, she did little things that were sort of annoying, but I just brushed them off—they didn't get to me. Now, I'm afraid I'm blowing this relationship—or will, if this keeps up."

After checking a few more areas of his life, I decided it was time for me to approach the subject of spirit possession. The clues seemed to point in that direction; the suddenness of the onset of his symptoms, the uncharacteristic behavior and the mental problems; his inability to concentrate, comprehend and remember. It sounded like spirits whose ages or mental development would have precluded their admission to college.

I told Tony that I thought he might have one or more entities with him who were complicating his life. He accepted the idea immediately and readily agreed to the depossession.

I prepared him for hypnosis, answered a few questions, and covered him with the lavender plaid blanket I use with patients as he stretched out in the chair which was now reclining.

He relaxed immediately when I began the hypnotic induction. As it continued, his body and facial muscles appeared to let go of all the tension I had witnessed earlier.

After I obtained a baseline of how *he* was reacting to hypnosis, I addressed any entities that might have been with him. Suddenly, his body became rigid, his face contorted, and he started shaking. When I informed them that their loved ones had come to help and then told them to go with them to the spirit world, I hoped to see the usual changes indicating they had left. Instead, his body and face registered even more fear. I guessed that someone was badly frightened and needed extra help.

"Tell me what you're aware of, Tony."

"I see a young girl, maybe twelve. I saw her once in an accident. She wants to go with an older woman who's come for her . . . but she's afraid—doesn't know what to expect."

I then talked directly to the girl and painted a picture of the spirit world and the friends she would have, and her perfect spirit body.

"She doesn't want to leave *me*."

"Tell her you don't want her to stay with you."

There was a long silence, and then his body relaxed and he smiled broadly.

I gave him hypnotic suggestions to come out of the trance, and asked him what had happened.

"At first I was really angry, and I said mentally, 'Get out of here *now!* Just leave!' And I felt a 'No, I won't!' It was automatic. And I then talked to her like I would to a child, 'You have to go. It will be good for you.' Then I could feel she accepted it and left. And I felt kind of light and really good. I feel like I want to go ahead and start school again—I want to catch up now."

In order to learn more about his susceptibility to possession, I decided to regress him to the time the spirit joined him. He slipped back into a deep trance as I began the hypnotic induction, and after being given suggestions to regress to a few minutes before she possessed him, he recalled visiting Dr. Adams at his office during a break from college. He was reading a magazine in the waiting room when he became alert to something happening outside.

Tony. I hear . . . a sound. It's like a bump, and I think it might be a car accident, but I didn't hear any screeching tires. I hear this girl saying, "Oh, my God! Oh, my God! Help me! Help me!" And I turn around and look outside . . . and I see somebody running across the street, back and forth. So I get up and I run into the hall . . . and ask the secretary to call the highway patrol and tell them there's an accident . . . and call an ambulance also.

I run outside. It's raining. I run around the building to the street . . . and I still see the girl running back and forth. I stop in the street to make sure there are no cars coming . . . and a truck goes in front of me, and then I cross. I see two people standing there . . . a man on the left side, and an older lady on the right . . . and there's a body on the street.

And first it looked like it was an old lady . . . and a gentleman's kneeling down now . . . and there's blood all around her head on the pavement. I walk . . . and I think I should go and help her. But I don't want to move her. But then I feel really scared . . . I don't want to see . . . I don't want to see how she looks . . . because I saw the blood . . . and I saw it was right around her head. But I want to go help the girl. I feel like I *should* do something!

So I walk over and I just sit there and look at her . . . and I see the ambulance come . . . and I leave. I feel relief that someone else is there to help. And I walk back into the building . . . A few minutes pass . . . and then I go back outside and I stand across the street . . . and I watch them pick up the girl. I notice her legs, just dangling down, and I feel terribly upset! They put her on the gurney, and all the blood on it got soaked up really fast. (Long pause.)

Now, I'm seeing myself . . . When I read about it in the paper, it hit me like I ran into a wall or something, when I find out she died! And I see myself talking to my parents and explaining to them about her, and I'm *so* upset about it! And I'm usually not this upset about things like that.

DR. FIORE. Now go to the very moment her spirit actually joined you.

TONY. I feel there were two times! One time . . . standing on that street . . . I feel like I was the only person there with an experience that came close to what was happening to her, and she grabbed onto me. And the other moment, when I was reading that newspaper, realizing that she died at the hospital. (Long pause.) I'm feeling tense again. God, I feel like I did right before I got hit in my accident. I'm just waiting for it to happen. Now I feel myself rolling in my car. I keep flashing back to the girl when she got hit . . .

This is something totally different now. I see myself when I was sixteen years old in the hospital, a long time ago, in the Emergency Room. An old lady was brought in. I heard the doctors say she was having a heart attack. They were trying to help her, but she died in the bed right next to me. Then one made a joke about her, and another one said, "Well, we lost that one!" I don't know why I remember that. It bothered me! (Long pause.)

Dr. Fiore. Just speak out whatever comes to mind.

Tony. I think the person who died is the type of person who's always trying to bring other people down. And I feel . . . it's almost like a—as if . . . she knew I was there. And wanted to bring me down by doing what the other girl did to me.

Dr. Fiore. By possessing you?

Tony. Yeah. That's what happened.

Dr. Fiore. Do you think she left with the depossession?

Tony. No. I can feel her with me now. (Long pause.) You know, I can sense that it was almost like she was not with me all the time. It's very strange, because now I remember clearly when that time happened. And I feel like . . . she came and went. And I didn't like that feeling. Because I felt like I didn't have any control over it at all. I felt at those times that I didn't want to do anything! . . . That's when she was there. (Long pause.) It makes sense now. (Long pause.) I'm still feeling a little confused.

Dr. Fiore. Now I'm going to speak to her. (Pause.) Remember when you had a heart attack? Perhaps you don't even realize you did. Well, your physical body died then—in the hospital. There was this young boy there. He was hurt and in the bed next to you. For some reason you went over to him . . . and you've been with him ever since.

I easily convinced the remaining spirit to leave, especially after offering her a youthful, healthy body that would serve her needs during her stay in the spirit world.

Once out of hypnosis, Tony stretched and then reported, "She mellowed out really fast. At first, I didn't like her personality—she was bitter and angry. But she listened carefully to what you told her, and I could feel her change. She had been with me over five years! I bet she's the one who's been giving my girlfriend a hard time. She was upset when you said she had died, and I felt sorry for her. But when she saw her husband come for her, she really felt happy, and left right away. That was neat!"

I explained to Tony that it seemed he was particularly vulnerable to possession, having picked up the two entities by feeling sympathetic and upset about what had happened to them. I urged him to surround himself daily with White Light (see chapter 15) and, additionally, to do so in any situation where there was negativity—fighting, arguing, pain, both mental and physical—or if he were around people using drugs and/or drinking.

We both felt a sense of having accomplished our mutual task, and agreed that the problem may have been resolved. Tony left the office a much happier and relieved young man.

I didn't hear from Tony for several months, which wasn't surprising, because I felt that we had stamped out the fires as we had hoped. I also knew that he was going into his final exams and would be caught in a time crunch. In fact, it was a very good sign that he hadn't called for another appointment. It suggested that he no longer needed my help.

Several months later, I began therapy with one of Tony's parents and had an opportunity to inquire about him.

"It's like night and day! He's been doing great since his visit here!"

I decided Tony's case would be particularly interesting because he was able to solve his problem in just one session—which is relatively unusual. Also, there were other unique aspects that would be helpful for readers to know about; the fact that he had picked up two spirits so very easily, mainly because of his sympathy for them, and that both could leave him and return at will.

I decided to phone him to hear directly about his improvement. After a month of calls to each other's answering machines, we finally made contact one evening.

"It's amazing! I saw you on a Friday and had an anatomy

class on the following Tuesday and barely had time to study, crammed in two weeks' worth over the weekend and Monday, and did really great—a B! It's the best score I've gotten since the problem started. I'm surprised at how I can read and concentrate now. It's neat to be able to study again."

"Tony, is there any trace of the problem?"

"Sometimes I feel it about to happen—not very often—and I stop it. It's like I'm pushing it out. I'm getting progressively better at doing that."

When I asked him about his exams, he proudly told me he had graduated five days before! "What's best is that now I know I have the potential to do well."

I congratulated him and told him how happy I was that he had overcome his obstacles. I added, "Tony, I'm concerned about the fact that you have had even a twinge of the problem. It could mean that one of the entities did not go into the Light, but is hanging around you and is able to get to you once in a while. I think it would be wise for you to come in for another session sometime soon, especially since you'll be under pressure in medical school in the fall."

He agreed to make an appointment, and volunteered that he wasn't irritable with his girlfriend anymore and didn't jump at things. "You remember the old lady that died in the bed right next to me in the hospital when I was in high school? Since she left, there's no more explosions, and I feel calm."

"I'm sure I warned you, Tony, not to take *any* drugs or alcohol. You seem to pick up spirits very easily, like a magnet. Since you want to be a doctor, you have to make sure you are protected, as they may gravitate toward you, wanting your help. Take extra precautions with the White Light."

"If I have a beer, I do it at home. Last summer I was having some wine with Dr. Adams and his wife, and he said he could see my aura diminish, just shrink right in as I was drinking. He told me the other day that he had been really worried about me. He's real pleased now. *And* he wasn't surprised at all about the spirits."

"Did he see the spirits in your aura or body before?"

"No. But when the girl got killed, he didn't go outside for more than a few seconds, because he knew she'd committed suicide in a past life. He realized she was dead and would grasp onto something—so he went right back in. He felt he couldn't help her and needed to protect himself."

"You need to protect yourself, too," I emphasized, sensing this young man hadn't seen the last of spirits.

"They now have more difficulty getting to me. Last week I was driving by an accident, saw an ambulance and a person lying on the road. I thought about what you said, and Dr. Adams told me about it too. I imagined White Light around me. I felt the *strangest* sensation of something trying to get in—but stopping, not being able to."

I told him that I was glad he had remembered to do that and reminded him to do it daily, not just if or when he witnessed a tragedy.

"I do feel them get in, and I create an energy and push them out. They don't get in long enough to affect me. I don't want to ever go through that again! They just about destroyed me before."

We were concluding our conversation when Tony interjected that he noticed he was more perceptive of other people now, even thought he understood the "energy they're putting out."

And Tony is also more perceptive of himself. He now realizes some very important aspects of human and spirit behavior that will help him to be a fine, sensitive and effective healer.

8 * Case Study—Anne

"I even dream that my boss is trying to kill me!" Anne blurted out only five minutes into our first session. An attractive redhead in her mid-thirties, she was obviously distressed, fearing things had gone too far. She was on the verge of sacrificing her salary for relief from the intolerable strain at work.

Her casual attire—worn jeans and a soft green T-shirt—contrasted with the rigidity of her body. When she leaned forward in her chair, her chin started to quiver despite her efforts at remaining in control. Tears filled her eyes as she explained, "I have twelve years invested in the company and I've done a good job—as a project manager. I'm in a senior position now and respected by everyone, except Bill, my boss. For more than a year, his behavior's been unacceptable. He wants power over me—to control me. I refuse to let him."

She described a struggle that had escalated to the point where she finally told him she was going to leave the company because of him. "But that just made it worse," she said. "He reacted so strongly that his boss, overhearing Bill's tirade, suggested that it might be more comfortable for him to work in another department. But Bill wouldn't hear of that!"

Reaching for a tissue, Anne added, "I've worked for him for a total of two years. The first six months were fine—a real friendship. That's the problem. He got to know all about me. I think he's jealous of my capabilities and the successes in my personal life. Then, the tables turned very quickly."

"How do your coworkers see the relationship, Anne?"

"They talk about him all the time and tell me that I'm right—that he harasses me. He's taken away most of my responsibilities. He's turned me into a secretary—just tells me to put memos on the PC [personal computer] without even asking for feedback. Little by little, he's chipped away at my self-esteem."

Now she was crying openly. "I've really suffered!"

I suggested that she sit back and relax and, when she was calmer, I asked her about her home life. She finally smiled. "I have a wonderful husband! He's been very supportive through all this. Whatever I decide to do is okay with him. He's even agreed to sell the house, if need be, so I won't have to work for a year or so while I pull myself together."

Wondering if her reaction to Bill was a reflection of an earlier relationship with her father, I asked her about him.

"I've always gotten along fine with Dad. We're real close." Then she summarized her past relationships with men, and it seemed to me that this situation with Bill was unique.

I wanted to know if she was aware of my work with past lives, as I suspected that the roots of her problems went back to another lifetime. "Why did you select me as your therapist?"

"I've been doing a lot of soul-searching for the past six months—and wondered if we knew each other before—you know, in an earlier life. You worked with Grace, a friend of mine, and she thought you could help me. Do you think it's possible that Bill and I have been together before?"

"Anne, whenever we have a relationship with someone, we have been with them *many* times before, especially if it's intense. You've been with your husband maybe hundreds of times, in many roles, even as a male. You may have been his father, and he your daughter. You can tell a lot about what you've worked out before, by the quality of the relationship now. If it's harmonious, you can be pretty sure that, at least in the last few times together, you've had good relationships. If there's conflict, as there is with Bill, then you've had problems, maybe *much* worse. You and Bill have tangled before! We'll have to get back to that time to help you get rid of the charge you have with him; then you won't have any buttons for him to push."

Since Anne seemed unable to cope with her relationship with Bill, which didn't fit with her obvious competence and achievements, I decided to broach the subject of possession. She was aware that I did past-life therapy, but she may not have known about my work with spirits. However, I wanted to go through my mental checklist first.

"How are your memory and concentration?" Her answer to this would be important.

"I never used to have any problems with my memory. I was noted for my perfect recollection. It's been getting progressively worse this past year, but I noticed changes even three years ago. And since I gave up smoking last year, I've had a real problem concentrating. Cigarettes used to calm me down."

I asked her about hospitalizations, surgical operations or accidents.

"I was hit by a car when I was almost three and was in a coma for a few months. Then four years ago, I was injured in an auto accident. I'm still in therapy for that. Otherwise, I've never been in the hospital."

I eased into the topic of spirit possession and my work in this area and noticed that her chin was quivering again. "What are you feeling right now?"

"I can *hear* my heart pounding!" she replied, tears starting to run down her face.

She was ready for hypnosis! An entity was upset and I could have contacted him or her immediately. Just to be on the safe side that it wasn't Anne herself reacting, I decided to follow my usual sequence and get a baseline by making her a relaxation tape.

I educated her a little about hypnosis and suggested that she push the chair to a reclining position, close her eyes, and begin to concentrate on her breathing. I then gave her soothing and positive hypnotic suggestions, which I recorded for her to listen to as she drifted off to sleep at night. She seemed beautifully relaxed, her head falling to her shoulder.

After turning the tape over to the opposite side, I recorded the depossession. Within seconds of addressing any spirits that may have been with her, I noticed a distinct shift from a blissful expression to one of total agitation—a "violent" reaction. There was my evidence! Her crying was so strong that I almost discontinued the recording. However, I invited in the spirit's loved ones, as I routinely do, and witnessed the entity calming down. I continued and shortly observed the tension in her body abruptly release. I ended the depossession and brought her out of trance.

"He didn't want to go," she reported, starting to cry softly. "I don't know why, but I feel sad."

"What else are you aware of?"

"I can feel a fluttering here." She pointed to her chest. "When he doesn't feel threatened, everything calms down."

"Could you tell who it is?"

"A man. For some reason, I feel sure it's a man. I don't know who, though."

Since he probably had not left, I asked her to close her eyes again, and to monitor the reactions she felt as I talked specifically to that spirit. Tears streamed down her face as I pointed out how hard it was for a man to be trapped in a female body. Then I invited him to go with his loved one, perhaps his mother, to the spirit world where he would be in his own strong, healthy, male body.

Seeing that Anne was relaxed again, I brought the depossession to a close.

"Could you feel him go this time?"

"I think he went with his mother. When you mentioned that maybe his mother was here for him, I could feel a change. My body felt suddenly calm."

"It may be that he left. If not, let's hope he will when you play the depossession tape. If he doesn't, I'll work with him some more during your next session. Play both sides of the tape daily. Use the depossession side when you're more alert, like in the early morning before work or early in the evening. The other side, which I've labeled 'sleep suggestions,' can be played as you drift off to sleep. Even if you don't listen to what I'm saying, your subconscious mind never sleeps and is absorbing every suggestion."

I checked the clock and saw that we still had forty minutes left of the double session. "We have time to do a regression to find out if you've been with Bill before. If so, we'll see if you can remember the event that is causing the tension between the two of you. The remarkable thing is that if you do, *he* may have a change of heart. I've seen that happen before. There must be a telepathic link between people that causes a reaction automatically. When you experience the past life, it not only heals you, but maybe him too, even without his knowing about the regression."

"That would be great! Do you think I can recall a previous incarnation?"

"It's not hard—if you don't try! Trying gets in the way. Just know that it's as easy as remembering something that happened yesterday. If you follow my directions, we'll get something worthwhile today—even if it's just practice."

I gave her instructions on how to report what would come to mind under hypnosis and answered a few questions about what a regression was like. Then I induced hypnosis and gave her suggestions to regress to that particular time when she and Bill had been together before that was having the greatest effect on her now.

After a little hesitation, she described a bucolic scene: a tree-lined dirt road with fields on either side. A young couple were walking hand in hand. She volunteered that it must be the late 1800s or early 1900s from the clothes and a carriage she saw. She said she thought the people were fond of each other and were enjoying their outing. I moved her ahead in time. She stated, without any emotion, that the relationship had ended. Knowing from experience that something traumatic probably had occurred that she didn't want to remember, I gave her suggestions to overcome the resistance.

"They're having an argument . . . hands lashing out . . . beating on him!"

"Tell me more about it."

"It's pretty violent. She's screaming. He's throwing her to the ground. She's crying. (Long pause.) My mind is blank. They're gone!"

At this point, I decided to try another tack that I've used as a trump card when necessary. "Tell me your dream again: the one of Bill killing you."

"There are some trees and a library in a small town . . . and a couple. (Pause.) The same couple! . . . He killed me! *He killed me!*"

She covered her face with her hands and muffled loud sobs

and groans. "With his bare hands. Oh, my God! I don't want to know any more!"

I appealed to the part of her that wanted to be healed and helped her to overcome her fears with reassuring suggestions.

"They're fighting with him, trying to stop him. Now he has something in his hand . . . and he's beating me with it—*over and over!*" She was shaking violently as she remembered her death. Suddenly she stopped—all the torment gone. "It's over. (Long pause.) I feel very light . . . and now I feel like I'm floating up."

"Look down and tell me what you see."

"I see the girl lying there."

"And he?"

"He's almost happy. Some ladies are trying to help me . . . but it's over. He's just standing there."

Realizing that she must remember the reason for the argument, I regressed her to the beginning of the fight—before he touched her.

"He's accusing me of something."

"What?"

"Of being with another man. (Long pause.) This *other* man! *The one in my body!*" She opened her eyes, bringing herself abruptly out of trance, and sat up. "That's what it is!"

Since she needed to come to terms with all that she had learned, I decided not to do any more work with the spirit at this time. I wanted to know how she felt—she had been through a great deal in one session—and her first at that!

"I feel different! Strong!" A beautiful smile lit up her face.

What a triangle we had!

I hardly recognized Anne when I went to call her from the waiting room for her second session. She was the picture of a professional woman, stylishly dressed in a good-looking suit. Her makeup put the finishing touches on the overall appearance of perfect grooming.

She walked confidently into my office, smiling pleasantly. "I'm much better. I can't believe it! My husband even noticed that my driving is different. I used to be a very aggressive driver, but now I'm much more relaxed."

"Well, Anne, what about work?"

"Because of the holiday, I've just been back for a half-day, but my whole approach toward my boss is different. It changed immediately. Bill actually came and talked to me in a much more social way. I noticed him watching me, with a surprised look on his face.

"I feel different toward myself. I have lots more energy and am putting lots more effort into myself."

I asked her if she thought the spirit had left. She nodded and answered that she was pretty sure he had. After a pause, she commented that she felt a surge of heat when I asked that question, and then realized that it was not hot in my office.

I sensed that her reaction was probably the entity partially manifesting because of my question. Perhaps he was reliving his death, which might have involved fire. I decided to check it out. I shared my suspicions with her, and placed her under hypnosis to explore their relationship in the same past life we had tapped into last time.

She recalled that she and the man were in love. They had talked about making love, but decided to run away together first. After laughingly plotting their "escape," they planned to rob a safe . . . Bill's safe. "We were going to steal his money—take it and leave."

Sneaking into a building at night, her boyfriend went to light a stick of dynamite, while she hid in the bushes outside. There was a loud explosion and she saw the building on fire. "Something went terribly wrong!" With a great deal of agitation, and tears streaming down her face and neck, Anne continued, "He was killed in the explosion! People came running to put the fire out, and I joined them, but I had to mask my emotions."

After continuing the regression a few minutes more to a time when she was not upset, I brought her back to the present, then I asked her to speak out loud to the spirit and tell him in her own words that she wanted him to leave now. Crying hard, she did and then "confessed" that he had stayed because she wanted him to. He left telling her that he felt it was time for him to go.

I asked her how she felt.

"I miss him," she whispered.

Anne came out of hypnosis with my suggestions to feel fine in every way, fully awake and alert. Although teary-eyed, she smiled tiredly.

Then, looking puzzled, she asked, "How could he be a spirit now? It was a long time ago. Do spirits stay here *that* long?"

I explained that only he could answer that question. I added, "He probably reincarnated. After his last death, he remained earthbound and was attracted to you because of your past-life bonds."

We set up her next appointment for two days later and she left, saying that she felt much better.

As I reviewed my notes before I went to the waiting room for Anne, I felt we had made tremendous progress in our two meetings. If her improvement had continued, I would suggest that this would be our last appointment. Anne had come for one specific problem, and if it were resolved, there would be no need for further help.

One look told me that my optimism had been premature.

Collapsing into the chair, she shook her head. "I don't know what's happening to me! I felt so up after our first session."

"Are you having problems with your boss?"

"No, that's great! Even though he's given me lots of reasons to be upset, he doesn't bother me at all!"

She went on to explain that she had been fine until that morning. She awoke after having one of the best night's sleep in a long time. When she had been up for a few hours, she couldn't see well, and it got increasingly worse. She became so dizzy she was close to passing out and vomiting. After calling in sick, she went back to bed, getting up at noon to go to work because she needed to finish a project that was due. At the office, she couldn't concentrate. After one hour of pushing herself, she gave up and went home. She went right to bed and slept until it was time for her to leave for our appointment. She commented, "As we were driving to your office, I got dizzy again."

"Were you driving?"

"Yes."

"Why didn't you let your husband take over?"

"I was alone."

"I thought you said 'we.' "

"I did? I wonder why I said that."

"Have you ever experienced this dizziness before?"

"I've had two migraines in my life, one eleven years ago and the other eight years ago. They started exactly the same way I felt this morning. I had pain both times that was so bad it felt like my head would crack open. Nothing I could do or take would relieve it. I even lost my peripheral vision. I was afraid I would get that pain this time. Thank God, I didn't."

When she was under hypnosis, I regressed her to the event responsible for the dizziness. She recalled a previous life as a male in which she had been a high-ranking officer in the Spanish military. There had been a political upheaval, and he and his followers were overthrown. Because of his position, he was exiled to a remote island. After being there for some time, living in fear of his enemies coming after him, he spotted a ship approaching the island.

At this point in the regression, she started to become upset and slipped into reliving it, rather than just reporting the details.

As a small group of men—a captain and his sailors—approached the cave in which he lived, he became very alarmed, knowing they meant to kill him if he didn't give them some vital information.

"We're talking loudly to one another. They want something, but I'm not going to give it to them. The one in charge is ordering them to kill me. (She was about to lose control, reexperiencing his panic.) They hit me on the back of the head with the butt of the gun and I fall to the ground. (Long pause.) I'm dizzy . . . very dizzy. I'm losing consciousness . . . all I see is red. It's my blood. I feel real tired . . . they just keep hitting me. (Long pause.) I see the person on the ground. (Long pause.) I don't feel tired anymore . . . I don't feel part of that anymore."

Now that she had dealt with the event that probably had caused the prior migraine problem and associated dizziness, I decided to find out who the "we" were. Her slip of the tongue was a dead giveaway that she had someone else with her. It was also possible that the entity we had worked with during the last two sessions had not left.

She was still deeply hypnotized and enjoying being in the Light following the death she had relived. I asked her what she meant by "we."

"There are others with me. They control me. They are very concerned that you might try to make them leave. They are very strong, and angry with you now that I know about them being with me."

I regressed her to the moment they joined her. She relived being on the operating table when she was a child, after being hit by the car.

"Something sharp, metal, has cut me. The back of my head hurts. The doctors are panicky. I'm hardly breathing. This goes on for quite a while. I'm going deeper and deeper. My arms hurt. It's hard to breathe . . . my chest is very heavy and my leg hurts . . . I'm going deeper. I'm having trouble breathing. I feel like I'm barely alive . . . That's when another person comes with an old, dark, wrinkled face. There are three of them. They take over. I feel real warm when they take over. They make my body feel better. They make the pain go away."

"Did you agree that they could take over?"

"No, they just came. Two women and one man. The man is very old and very tired."

I then spoke directly to them, telling them their work was over. They had saved the life of the little girl—thirty-one years ago—but she was well now. They needed to think of their own welfare and to go with the loved ones who had come for them. All three left within seconds.

Once out of hypnosis, Anne explained that she had been running across the street in front of her home to join her mother when she was hit by a car. She was taken to the hospital and remained in a coma for several months—and was not expected to live. Her parents were told that if she survived, she would never be normal, wouldn't be able to communicate with anyone, and probably would have to live in the Children's Hospital all of her life.

Anne grinned as she said, "Maybe they not only pulled me through, but helped me to develop normally. They meant well!"

Anne's fourth and last session was five days later. She almost bounced into my office, looking radiant. Things were going extremely well at her work. Her boss went out of his way to explain things and was much more flexible. She was surprised that she didn't talk about him behind his back any longer. If others brought up criticisms about him, she let them drop—almost automatically. She said that everything before—all of the depression, thoughts of leaving and selling the house—were like a dream now, fading from her awareness. In fact, she had felt really good since our last session. She had lots more energy, which she saw as a real benefit.

I suggested it would be helpful for her to explore her relationship with Bill, since that had been her ticket of admission to my office. I felt we didn't really know much about who they were to each other—just that he had killed her. She agreed and with a guilty smile said, "I'm really curious how he found out about the other man."

I regressed her to the moment Bill discovered her involvement with her lover.

"The night of the explosion . . . some horses are coming up with a wagon. It's Bill. He asks me what happened. The house is burning. He's screaming, 'What happened?' People are running around trying to put the fire out. He's running around now giving orders to people and I'm feeling real bad . . . I think they found the body. Yes, we all did. I'm looking at it also. He's looking at the safe. It's open and he's finding out what's missing. He looks at everyone in the room. He notices me. He always trusted me. (Long pause.) I was like a sister to him. We grew up in the same family. (She cries.) That's why he trusted me so much. We were raised together. He's looking at me suspiciously. He finds it hard to believe, though, but yet there's enough doubt."

I asked her what she is feeling.

"I never should have betrayed him. He trusted me," she answered, crying hard.

She continued the regression, describing how he had taken care of and protected her—smothering her with his devotion. After the fire, she wanted to move to another town, but he refused to give his permission. Sometime later she confronted him as they were coming out of church one Sunday, telling him she was definitely leaving. He argued with her about it. She was adamant. He became irrational, to the point of "going crazy" and finally attacking her. She relived her death again, adding that she realized she didn't want to live as he was beating her. She escaped from her guilt and the trap she felt she was in by slipping out of her body.

As we were concluding our session, Anne commented, "I've wondered why I just didn't wait it out, instead of coming for help. He's going to be gone for three months to set up another sales office in Japan—and he's leaving in only two weeks! If I'd waited, none of this would have happened, because the pressure would have been off."

"Anne, I've come to the conclusion that everyone seeks help at the very time that is best. *There are no accidents!* If you had waited, four lost souls would still be imprisoned here on the earth plane, and you and Bill would not have made your peace, which probably is one of your purposes in this lifetime. You've healed yourself spiritually, and you've helped him. I wonder if there weren't highly evolved beings, your guides, who inspired you to give yourself a chance to be freed from not only the possessions, but also the negative memories from the past."

The problem appeared to be resolved, and we both agreed this would be our last time together, unless something else came up.

9 ✲ *Case Study—Peter*

This is one of the most fascinating of all my cases of possession, perhaps because it did not lend itself to a quick and easy resolution. As a result, the case fully demonstrates the intriguing interplay of the possessing spirits' personalities and problems with those of the possessed patients. In addition, the case of Peter is particularly interesting because of the sheer number, persistence and variety of spirits that found temporary lodging with him.

I first met Peter when he came to my office early in the fall of 1983, having been referred by a friend who knew of my work. He was hoping for some psychological counseling—with the possibility of exploring a past life—as a means of tackling his many personal problems.

Peter was a tall, muscular thirty-five-year-old with a mustache, jet-black hair and dark eyes. He immediately struck me as a person suffering from dejection, fear and guilt. He had the air of a trapped animal as his eyes studiously avoided mine and shifted quickly about the office.

As I heard the details of his life during our first few sessions, it became clear that every area was in chaos.

A computer analyst, Peter had moved quickly up the ladder into a staff position to a vice president. Despite his accelerating success, his emotional and personality problems were undermining his self-confidence and threatening his career. He described himself as a "bundle of nerves." He was especially anxious and scared in groups. This was a problem for him because he was required to give regular briefings to top executives of his own and other companies.

He spoke of frequently having severe anxiety attacks before meetings, and once—in a blind panic—actually running out of a room full of executives. He described several other anxiety attacks he had suffered while driving in rush-hour traffic in San Francisco, during which he actually had to pull to the side of the street for fear of passing out. These attacks manifested the full range of physical symptoms, from palpitations and sweats to nausea and dizziness.

Peter spoke of many times when he had juggled his schedule to avoid the dreaded briefings, all the while knowing that he was depriving himself of opportunities for advancement, as well as failing in his responsibilities to his employers. At other times, however, he functioned brilliantly in important meetings, speaking and behaving with complete self-confidence and aplomb. When I asked him to explain why he was so erratic, he was at a total loss.

Another problem bothered him even more deeply. He had a growing inability to concentrate and remember details and claimed his memory was reduced by fifty percent. He frequently lost his train of thought in conversations and couldn't keep his mind on work or reading for more than five minutes at a time. To make matters worse, on many evenings he was unable to recall whole segments of his day; hours at a time would be a complete blank. He could account for them only by referring back to the daily records or by asking his workmates what they had done.

Because of increasing fears of failure, Peter had begun to procrastinate in his work, and he was convinced that if he kept going on as he was, he would end up insane.

To add to his dilemma, he was also chronically incapable of getting along with women. He was on his third marriage, which was failing rapidly. He was no longer sexually attracted to his wife, Betty, although he claimed she was physically beautiful. He was terrified that perhaps he was a repressed homosexual. At the same time, he was fanatically jealous of Betty and resented the interest that men took in her when they were at parties. He often accused her of flirting, and this sometimes led to nasty near-physical confrontations. Afterward he felt guilty and full of remorse.

As Peter became more comfortable with me, he admitted that he was worried about his drinking. Heavy drinking had been a major part of his life for years. He drank almost every day and viewed drinking as the one real relief he had from his fears and anxieties.

Though brought up in an upper-middle-class family with a banker for a father, Peter had always preferred drinking among working men in the rougher sorts of establishments. When drinking, his ordinarily pleasant disposition turned sour. He would become extremely sarcastic and frequently started barroom brawls.

Because of what I've learned about the relationship between drinking and the entry of spirits, my suspicions were growing stronger about the possibility of possession as the cause of his problems. Also, I had carefully noted the odd duality that ran through most of the problem experiences of his life. He loved his wife, yet he was not attracted to her and treated her badly. He was compassionate and loving, yet he had a terrible temper and occasionally took out his wrath on innocent pets, playmates, friends and lovers. He was highly competent in his work, yet he felt dull-witted and unworthy.

In addition to these suggestive personality traits and symptoms, Peter had had several distinct experiences that seemed to be strong clues supporting the hypothesis of possession. I've found that highly sensitive people are particularly prone to possession, and as a child he had had several psychic experiences. In the first grade he foresaw a dog attack that actually took place a few days later. Years later he had a premonition of the suicide of a favorite aunt.

Peter admitted feeling ruled frequently by two different personalities, one benign and one malevolent. From childhood he had recurrent nightmares of a wizened, evil man glaring at him.

He recalled that throughout his life in sports, every time he had an opportunity to make a major success, he would hurt himself. He badly injured a knee while trying out for the college varsity football team. In high school, injured shoulder ligaments had kept him from the state wrestling championship.

Frequently, when he was speaking with someone, he would get the feeling that another being was speaking through him. He even felt sometimes that he wasn't really occupying his body at all, but as though he'd "stepped back and to the left from my head about one foot."

That feeling immediately reminded me of similar comments by other patients who had indeed turned out to have been possessed.

During our third session I suggested that we use hypnosis to check for possessing entities. Peter seemed alarmed at the prospect, despite my careful explanation of the concept of possession and how important a depossession could be. Hesitantly, he agreed to try.

He proved to be an extremely good hypnotic subject. He went into hypnosis quickly and easily and accepted my finger-signal communication system. A check by finger signals immediately indicated that he did have a number of spirits with him—six or more—and when I asked if any of them had been with him since childhood, the "yes" finger lifted.

I did a simple depossession, after which his finger signals conveyed that at least three entities still remained. I then asked him to let me speak with the remaining entities and took my usual approach:

"Why are you imposing yourself upon this man's life, causing him problems, when you know that you have gone through the change called 'death' and should be progressing in your own spirit lives?" I asked.

Two different replies came, quite distinct in tone. One was something I had heard many times before from possessing entities: "I'm frightened," a trembling voice whispered. "I don't know what will happen to me. I don't want to go."

But the other reply surprised me with its brief but harsh sarcasm. "So what!" Suddenly I was very much aware that Peter and I had our work cut out for us.

I paused for a moment and then went through my standard depossession procedure again, explaining in detail the nature of spiritual experience, the learning and healing that would take place in the spirit realm, and then invoking close spirit friends or relatives to help us.

Before bringing Peter out of the hypnotic trance, I did a quick finger-signal check for entities. It proved negative; according to his subconscious mind there were no more spirits in his aura or body.

Once out of trance he said that he felt relaxed and refreshed. He commented that he had the distinct feeling that one of the entities had been very strong. He left feeling extremely optimistic.

At the beginning of our next session, a week later, Peter reported feeling much better. He was still suffering from anxiety, but less acutely, and his relationship with his wife seemed to have improved somewhat.

He appeared disappointed when I suggested that we do another check for spirits. I explained that often entities would only appear to leave on the first try and that sometimes others "came out of hiding" only gradually.

He quickly entered a trance and, as I had suspected, finger signals indicated that there were indeed more with him.

This time, I quickly established contact with one who gave his name clearly as Joseph Biddle and knew exactly why he was with Peter: "I hate him and I'm going to make him pay for what he's done to me."

"You're hurting yourself as well," I countered.

"I don't care. It's worth it as long as I can make him pay."

I asked Joseph to go back to the time of his death. He told of being alone in a Kansas hospital. He was angry when he died. Apparently he had married a younger woman who had borne him a child, but she had run away with the baby. He had carried the pain of that experience through the rest of his life and felt particularly bitter toward babies.

I asked Joseph to move to the time his spirit left his body. He told of seeing his wasted corpse lying in the bed, staying near it for some time, then moving through the hospital corridors.

"I see a tiny baby, a newborn. I think perhaps it's my baby. And I know that I can make the baby pay for leaving me. I join the baby. I have been with him ever since."

I knew immediately that this was a very important entity in Peter's life, and could possibly explain his periodic rages and cruelty.

I patiently explained to Joseph the jeopardy of his spiritual situation: how he was simply extending his own misery as well as inflicting misery upon a living human being who had nothing to do with his problems. I called upon friendly spirits to help guide him. Soon Joseph saw his sister and departed with her.

Before bringing Peter out of hypnosis I was able to make contact with one more spirit. Unlike Joseph Biddle, this one was unclear about who he had been or what he was doing with Peter—in fact, he was befuddled, almost in a stupor.

"C'mon, let's have a drink," the entity kept repeating jovially. "Let's go down to Rocky's and have some fun."

I was able to learn that he had been a heavy equipment operator in his past life, with an obvious fondness for the bottle. He had apparently been with Peter since his early childhood. The last thing he was able to remember of his life was using a Caterpillar tractor on a construction site.

It took little urging for him to depart.

When Peter was out of hypnosis, we discussed the latest findings. He felt strongly that Joseph Biddle had exerted a major influence upon his life. He recalled his early dream images of a hostile old man. He was less sure about the Caterpillar operator. We agreed that perhaps that entity could explain his drinking and his fascination with the rough, working-class style. He left that session feeling hopeful and enthusiastic.

However, in our next session the Caterpillar operator surfaced immediately when Peter went into a trance.

"You're still here. What's your name?" I asked.

"Lou, I think."

"But why are you still here with Peter?"

"He lets me drink. He can be fun, and I can get him to go to my kind of places."

"What kind of places?"

"You know, a place that's got real men in it who know how to drink—not a bunch of stuffed shirts."

"You've been with Peter a long time, haven't you?"

"Yes, I guess so."

"But you know you must leave, don't you?"

"Why?"

I explained the situation to him since he was obviously confused and thought he was still alive in his own body. Again, I brought him to the moment of his death in his last life. He described an accident in which the Caterpillar rolled on him.

"You were killed in that accident."

"I was?" he replied incredulously.

"What happened after that?"

"I saw a small boy playing in a backyard. He seemed pleasant enough and friendly. And I felt lonely—and lost. So I went toward him."

It finally became clear to Lou what had really happened. He said he was sorry for the harm he had done to Peter and asked how he could move on. I told him to look around to see if there was anyone he knew. He saw his wife, who he thought had died hating him for his drinking. Realizing she had forgiven him, he happily left with her. This time I had the feeling that he was gone for good.

I felt hopeful that we may have gotten to the root of Peter's problems and I told him so.

He smiled weakly. "I hope so too," he said, "but something funny happened when I was coming out of hypnosis this time. Something inside of me, some part of me, seemed to laugh. I couldn't tell if it was just my imagination or what. But it seemed to say, 'I've fooled you again, you still haven't found out I'm here.' "

Peter left wondering whether he was ever going to get any help from this approach. As he left, I found myself wondering if he would stick with the treatment long enough to reach the cure that was possible.

At our next session he smiled as he told me how much better he had felt that week—especially because he had had virtually no desire to drink. Frowning, he said that his lack of sexual desire for his wife was putting a real strain on his marriage. I promptly suggested hypnosis and, after so much practice, Peter quickly went into a deep trance.

At first, when I asked if there were any spirits present, his finger signals indicated a "no," but when I asked if any were "hiding," a "yes" answer came.

"May I speak to you?" I asked.

"She's not ready to speak to you, she's afraid," said Peter in a drowsy monotone.

"Tell me about her then."

"She's blond, pretty, but shy and quiet. She's very lonely. She doesn't know why she is so unhappy; she thought she would like it with me, but she doesn't like having sex with my wife. She hates that!"

"Do you know how long she's been with you?"

"I don't think so."

"Perhaps she'll talk to me."

Peter was silent, and I waited. After a minute I asked, "Is the female who is with Peter willing to speak now?"

"Yes, I'm here," came Peter's voice, yet softer, more hesitant, almost feminine.

"What's your name?"

"Laurie. But why am I here?"

"That's what we are going to try to find out, Laurie."

With gentle questioning, I was able to discover that this entity had met Peter at a party five years earlier, not long before he met his current wife.

She had been attracted immediately to him because of his dominant, aggressive nature. She remembered seeing him enter the party with a girl on each arm. Later she forced herself to walk up to him and introduce herself and they spent a half hour talking.

She died in a car wreck on the way home from that party.

I carefully explained to Laurie that by staying with Peter she was greatly retarding her own progress—and doing him immense harm.

She said, "I didn't realize that. I'm sorry."

"So, you must go. It will be far better for both of you."

"But I can't go. Where would I go? It's lonely."

I was about to do some more persuading when Peter said, "She won't go. She doesn't want to hear what you have to say. She won't listen to you any more."

I tried to communicate with her for several more minutes, but to no avail.

When he was out of hypnosis, Peter remembered having met Laurie. He was amazed that such a brief encounter could have led to her possessing him. But he recalled that soon after meeting Laurie, his feelings for women had undergone a gradual and subtle change.

We were now faced with the problem of somehow enticing Laurie to leave. Peter also said that as he was coming out of the trance, he had once again felt the presence of a strong malevolent personality that was mocking us.

Over the next few weeks, our sessions were not particularly noteworthy. We attempted to bring forth entities on several occasions with no success. Peter felt no underlying sense of alien presences whether under hypnosis or in his day-to-day life.

His sex life with his wife had improved. Things were going well for him at work, and he continued to have no desire for alcohol.

During these sessions, he elaborated on his inner feelings of worthlessness, guilt and insecurity. But generally, things seemed to be going so well for him that I was beginning to believe that he was no longer harboring spirits. Perhaps they had left spontaneously—on their own. Feeling his remaining problems could be helped with the ordinary tools of psychotherapy, I began to explore with him his early relationships with his father and mother.

However, during each session we continued to utilize a routine period of hypnosis with the hope of reestablishing contact with Laurie, and to check out the presence of any other entities.

Then in our first session in December, we unexpectedly made a breakthrough.

In the early minutes of the hypnotic trance, Peter's voice subtly changed its tone. "You still don't know I'm here, do you?" he gloated.

I immediately recognized the same mocking voice I had heard months earlier.

"How long have you been with Peter?" I asked, hoping to get an answer.

"Long enough to know him well—over four years."

"Why have you stayed with him for so long when you know you are only hurting him and yourself. You've had many chances to go in these past months."

"They would not like me. I've done some very evil things. If I went there I would have to change."

"But you do have to change. You cannot stay here. Look around you. Maybe there is someone you once knew who has come to get you. Do you see the Light?"

"I've seen the Light many times and I've seen my mother

near it. But I always run from it. I don't want to face her—and I'm afraid of what they would do to me."

"They wouldn't do anything to hurt you."

"I don't know."

Realizing I would get nowhere with this approach, I nonetheless felt encouraged that I had established a dialogue with this recalcitrant entity. I asked him to go back to his last lifetime. He said he lived in San Francisco with his mother around the turn of the century.

"My name is David," he said. "I don't remember what I did for a living, but I know that I practiced the black arts and gained much power through using them. I was the leader of a group who worshipped Satan. My mother never knew this. But she would hate me forever if she did. I destroyed many lives."

"You can be helped with all that later in the spirit world," I said. "But it is time to stop destroying lives now. Move ahead in time. Let yourself remember your death."

> The ground is shaking—an earthquake! Something just fell on my head, part of the building. I'm crushed by falling bricks! I see my lifeless body and I want to be back inside of it. I'm cheated out of life. (Long pause.)
>
> I saw the Light, which I've seen many times since, and I heard voices of people coming to get me. But I was afraid and I turned my back on them.
>
> The next thing I remember, I was with a man whose job was cleaning streets. I joined him to stay alive, although it wasn't a very good choice—and it was a terrible job. This man died a natural death—prematurely.
>
> After that I joined many, many people. I found I could join them when I wanted to and leave when I wanted to. It was interesting. When I got bored or depressed, I could just leave and find some other person to join.
>
> I made most of these people miserable. I gave them some power, some got very interested in the occult, but they all became depressed, and I didn't like to be around them for long.

"How did you join Peter?" I asked.

"He was drinking in a bar in San Francisco. He was with some friends, but he was withdrawn and unhappy. I could tell that he was weak and that it would be easy to join him. He had already known Satan."

When Peter and I discussed what had been revealed under hypnosis, he suddenly bowed his head in shame and told me that as a teenager he had been intrigued with the occult and had read several books on satanic rituals. He said that for years he had kept a small painted plaster statuette of a cloven-footed and bearded Satan on his dresser. On several occasions the figurine had bothered him emotionally, but he had been unable to bring himself to throw it away.

In our next session, I regressed Peter hypnotically to one of his past lives, and we discovered that he had indeed been an active Satan worshipper. This certainly helped to explain David's attraction to him.

In the following session I was able to make contact with David almost immediately and asked him, "Do you want to stay in this endless cycle, feeling miserable and causing misery in others when you know there is a way to stop it?"

"I am still afraid," he reluctantly replied.

I emphasized there was nothing to fear; any change would be a change for happiness and joy.

"But they hate me!"

"All that hate and shame is on your side—it's all in you. Your mother loves you. Look around, maybe she's here now."

Seconds passed. "Yes, here she is. She wants me to go with her and she forgives me. I'm going to go. Good-bye."

With that, the tortured entity, David, left.

Peter and I were both optimistic at the end of that session. Putting together the pieces of the puzzle, he could relate the period when David had joined him to greatly increased feelings of insecurity and self-hatred.

Over the next few weeks Peter's self-esteem continued to improve. He felt renewed confidence in himself and found that he was able to meet and work with people in his job with very little anxiety. His relationship with his wife was improving and his memory was far better.

During our sessions, we continued to use hypnosis as a check for the possible presence of entities. However, finger signals repeatedly showed there were none, so I used the remainder of the time under hypnosis to give him positive suggestions for improved self-esteem.

Toward the end of January, Peter appeared for his session in a nervous and uncomfortable state. He was on the verge of an anxiety attack that had started just before he left home to drive over to see me. As he got closer to my office building, he suffered from mounting fear and could almost hear a voice inside himself pleading for him to turn around and go back home. During the brief drive he suddenly developed a stuffy nose as though he had a bad cold. He had to muster all of his will power to enter my office and stay.

I put Peter into a trance immediately, thinking that David might have regained a foothold. Finger signals indicated that there was indeed a male entity present and that he wanted help. But instead of David, he turned out to be a lighthearted, fun-loving spirit named Eddie Vineburg, who said he was twenty-seven years old and had joined Peter at a Sacramento bar in 1978.

At first Eddie refused to admit that he was dead. When I asked him how he felt to be called "Peter," he replied blithely, "I'm a rock singer and people can call me anything they like, as long as they listen to my music and pay to hear it." He also managed to remark that he thought I was "foxy" and wouldn't mind a date with me!

It turned out that he had been a small-time singer who had played lounges and small clubs around Sacramento. He had burned to death in a car accident in 1978 immediately prior to joining Peter. He had been trapped in the car, and the last thing he remembered in that lifetime was inhaling thick pungent smoke that burned his nose and throat.

After the wreck, he stayed nearby, staring at his dead body. But the shock of seeing paramedics cart his charred body off in an ambulance had driven him away.

"I felt very lonely and lost then and headed back to the bar where I had been drinking before the wreck. But nobody would talk to me, and I couldn't even get a glance from any of the women. I felt like Caspar the friendly ghost!"

When he first saw Peter sitting at the bar, Eddie thought he looked like a "real schmuck," because he was so quiet and withdrawn. But he also sensed that he could easily join him. Out of loneliness he did.

I asked Eddie if he were ready to move on, and he said that he was. When I asked if he saw anyone there to escort him, he recognized a spirit aunt, Sylvia—and then he was gone.

Upon coming out of the trance, Peter felt fine, and all traces of the incipient anxiety attack had completely dissipated. Incredibly, the stuffiness in his nose was gone too. He recalled undergoing a minor personality change in 1978, suddenly taking an interest in bands and live singing that he had never had before. He also became quite a ladies' man and developed a newfound talent for picking up women and getting them to bed quickly.

At our next session, four days later, Peter reported that things were going fine for him professionally, and that his self-confidence was high. Yet his sexual problems with his wife had suddenly resurfaced with a vengeance. He found that he had absolutely no sexual desire for her—in fact he was repelled by the thought of making love with her. Whenever she touched him, he got upset. And she had complained that even in his sleep he would push her away.

Once in hypnosis, Peter's finger signals showed that there was, as I suspected, a female entity with him. It turned out to be Laurie, the girl who had died in the car wreck.

"Why are you still with Peter?"

"I feel trapped, and I'm afraid. I don't know where to go. It's so lonely here now because everybody's gone. But I can't stand his having sex with Betty."

"Are you ready to leave now?"

"Yes."

"Look around. Do you see anyone here for you? There is someone here."

"There's an old woman, a friend of my mother's. She's a . . . She delivered babies."

"A midwife?"

"Yeah."

"What does she say to you?"

"She says, 'C'mon on, girl, it's time to go now. Stop being so sad. It's time to start a new day.' I'm going with her now."

Since Peter's finger signals indicated that there were no more spirits with him, I brought him out of trance.

He remarked that he had experienced Laurie's immense joy at finally leaving. He added that she had felt abandoned by all the spirits who had left. They were the only company she had known.

Peter felt greatly relieved, as though a great weight had been lifted from him. He was convinced that he was finally free. But by now I had learned to take a "let's wait and see" attitude with him.

For several sessions following Laurie's departure, Peter reported that his sexual relationship with Betty had continued to improve. His self-confidence and work performance remained strong. And his drinking problem had vanished. It was time for us to terminate treatment. His goals had been accomplished.

Peter's intricate case demonstrates the complexities of the relationship between a living human being and earthbound spirits. His own past life as a Satanist had created a deep-seated guilt, which made him susceptible to possession. Each succeeding parasitic entity, starting with the bitter Joseph Biddle, simply weakened him more, increasing his vulnerability. The fact that at the age of five he was joined by the spirit of the alcoholic Lou only made the situation worse, because later—through his drinking—Peter continually opened his aura to more possessions.

He was prey to greatly troubled spirits. He became consumed with bitterness, fear and self-hatred. As he grew more possessed and troubled, he was less able to cope with life—professionally and personally. In the end, the possessing spirits were able to act out their personalities and drives directly through his behavior, while his own personality became increasingly overwhelmed and pushed to the side.

The road back to spiritual and psychological health for Peter was difficult and trying. It started with the dislodging of a single spirit. With each successive depossession, his own spirit grew stronger and more defined. His regression to the life as a Satanist helped him to release his deep-seated self-hatred and subconscious condition for possession.

With the final freedom from all possessing spirits, Peter was truly his own person and had made great steps along his spiritual path.

10 * Case Study—Barbara

"My weight has been a struggle for sixteen years. Ever since I had a total hysterectomy, it's been impossible to keep the pounds off. I've tried everything. I failed too often. I realize—*no more diets!*" Barbara had come to see me as a last ditch measure.

Indeed, it did seem she had tried everything! Her first diet was with Weight Watchers, and it took her eight agonizing months to lose thirteen pounds. Her next was supervised by a physician and consisted of shots of human gonadotropin and a five-hundred-calories-per-day regimen. She gained eight pounds—not cheating once! Then she sought help at a local diet center and was put on a protein "fast"—high-protein shakes and no solids. She lost thirty pounds. After a "bad weekend" of binges, she was afraid to return, expecting a scolding. The thirty pounds were back soon, plus a few extras! Then she went back to Weight Watchers and then later to another diet center. Nothing helped for long.

She had put off calling me for an appointment until she was desperate. A chronic depression, which she felt was intricately involved with her obesity, got the better of her, and she forced herself to take that first step.

Like most overweight patients, Barbara came for my help when she was at her highest weight—eighty pounds overweight. Down deep in her mind, she knew her therapy would be a soul-searching task and probably painful.

It's difficult for people to decide to reverse the defensive tactics of the mind and look within. With any symptom, there are traumas and hidden motives. Elaborate barriers are erected by their mind to protect the equilibrium, which often is impossible—at least to some degree.

Barbara was a lively, intelligent woman in her mid-forties. When I asked her what kind of work she did, she laughed and said, "I'm a jack of all trades, master of none!" Married for twenty-three years, she had two grown children.

It was obvious within minutes of our first session that she was a sensitive, caring and metaphysically minded person. She commented that she spontaneously remembered living in a temple in China as a mystic. Whether or not it was true, it suggested to me that she was on the spiritual path in this lifetime.

As a child, she suffered from nephritis. Hospitalized for three weeks, she was not expected to live. She remembered overhearing the doctors telling her mother that they didn't expect her to make it through the night. As sick as she was, she *knew* that she wasn't going to die.

Following that illness, she was extremely skinny. Her brother tormented her by bringing his friends to see her ribs! The family did everything they could to fatten her up—to no avail. She simply couldn't eat a complete meal. As she saw it, "I've had a weight struggle since the nephritis at seven!"

I felt that she had had many opportunities to be possessed. I discussed this with her, and she accepted the possibility. She added that besides the hospitalizations for the nephritis, hysterectomy and the childbirths, she had had her gall bladder removed twenty years ago.

She confirmed, "I feel spirits around me at night. I often sense something off to the left of me. I've wondered if it was the boy who used to live in our home. He was killed in a surfing accident just before we moved in. In fact, that's why his parents sold the house. There's one room, a bedroom, which I think was his. I can almost feel him in there."

Since patients' reactions to the depossession tape give me strong clues that help with the diagnosis of possession, I recorded one for her at that point.

As I was speaking to earthbound entities who might have been present, I noticed a lot of change in Barbara's facial expression, ranging from fear to delight. As I was finishing, her body and face relaxed considerably. I guessed that at least one spirit had left.

"I could see Billy, Ricky and Linda leave. I knew them back East. They seemed so glad to be going! I must have had them with me for years! Ricky died when we were both six!"

During our next sessions, she released many spirits, as I did depossession after depossession each time. In one, her finger signals indicated she had thirteen—many had joined her during her childhood illness. Some didn't realize that their bodies had died, others that their loved ones were there. A few times, I had to have them look into a mirror to see that they were not in their own bodies. Often, it was necessary to regress Barbara to the moment they joined her, to clarify who they were and why she had allowed them to incorporate. There was crying and trembling. Some were stubborn.

At times, the resistance was almost overwhelming. Someone was putting up a good fight! Barbara was about to cancel out completely on a number of occasions, and then miraculously realized that *she* didn't want to stop.

Each week she reported that there were times when she had more energy and noticed positive changes in her eating habits. The weight began to come off without dieting. But it was not all smooth sailing. There were setbacks when she was sapped of energy and felt inexplicably tired and sleepy. She also experienced assorted aches and pains. There were fears of many kinds that surfaced, ones she had had off and on for years. She sensed there were still people with her and could often feel some of them leave when she used the tape at home.

She summed it up, "I've been feeling good—and awful! Sometimes I felt raw. I've also had a need to be held, rocked and soothed, and I've been crying a lot."

One entity we had worked with came back. He hadn't gone into the Light. He took Barbara at her word that he could return, if he didn't like it. He needed to be helped to make a firm connection with his loved one, and then he finally left—for good!

She experimented by playing the depossession tape in the room that she thought had belonged to the young man who had been killed. It seemed that he left, because her reaction to the room changed and it appeared lighter to her. However, she sensed that her home was not cleared totally. Since then, I have suggested similar methods to other patients with good results.

As Barbara came in for her seventh session, I could see that things were not going well for her. She looked depressed, and her whole body reflected her mood.

"I'm discouraged! There's so much garbage in my life! I have a real feeling of helplessness. Many times, in the last couple of weeks, I've been so depressed that it takes all my conscious effort to pull myself up. I feel I'll never lose the weight—I'll die like this!"

"Have you thought of suicide?"

"Oh, yeah! It's been real strong. I *know* it's not me. I'm a real survivor! The first time it hit, I was forty. I got incredibly depressed. I felt the same way this past week. I even got sick, that's why I had to cancel my last appointment. I haven't been sick in a long time—at least a year. I created it to hide. I was exhausted, shaking, sweating! I slept twenty-four hours straight through. It's all tied in with the depression."

Under hypnosis, Barbara's finger signals indicated that she had an entity who had joined her when she was twenty—more than twenty-five years ago. When I asked if it was male, both the "yes" and "no" fingers lifted. Further questioning revealed that the spirit had been a homosexual female who had committed suicide.

Regressed to the woman's death, Barbara reported that she had jumped off the Golden Gate Bridge. Her face registered concern, and she said, "I know who she is—the daughter of a friend! I really liked her a lot. Such a neat person. I couldn't figure out why she was *so* unhappy. At first, I refused to believe she had committed suicide. Just before she did it, she wrote a letter to one of her friends telling him she was homosexual. Even her psychiatrist couldn't reach her."

I then asked her to remember when the entity took possession of her.

"When I took her picture home. I don't know why I asked her mother if I could keep it." After a long pause, she admitted that she couldn't remember her name. Immediately, a different voice came through, quietly saying, "Jean."

I wasted no time and spoke to her, calling her attention to

someone she loved dearly who had come for her. She left without further ado with her great-aunt.

Barbara announced, "We've been together—fighting!"

"What do you mean?"

"I would look in the mirror, and it wasn't really me I was looking at. Sometimes I felt very strange. *I never relaxed!* Always on edge. Fearful of heights. I was terrified of walking across the Golden Gate Bridge, which we did in 1979. I could have so easily crawled up there and gone over—again! I was not okay with myself. I had a strong identification with Jean."

After a pause, and looking puzzled, she reported, "They're still here, sitting and listening, Jean and her great-aunt."

I asked Barbara to speak directly to her, explaining she should go into the Light and the spirit world.

"It's almost like I invited you, Jean. I was envious of you. You were all I wanted to be. I knew you felt a lot of pain inside. I felt so bad when you committed suicide." Barbara continued to talk to her and finally persuaded her to go to the Light, which apparently she did.

"I didn't know who I was. I don't feel like I've ever felt the same since her death. She's been with me like a big burden for years. Now that she's gone, I feel an emptiness—like a cancer has been taken out. Something's been cut away, like I've had a costume on and now it's been taken off. A lot of tension's just been relieved.

"I feel strange—like there's another person here! She's the other person who was with Jean. She is very white and very heavy. She's so fat, she's like a big bubble. Her chin goes right down to her chest. She has almost orange-blond hair. (Long pause.) Margaret's her name. She was a friend of Jean's from high school. She had an attachment to Jean—in love with her. She killed herself . . . maybe because of Jean not returning her love the way she wanted it—physically. Then she possessed Jean."

So Jean was possessed at her death! Who really committed the suicide, Margaret or Jean? Maybe Jean's homosexuality, which she couldn't accept, drove her to kill herself. Or was it the spirit acting out? All these hypotheses were flashing into my mind as I asked Barbara what Margaret was feeling.

"Lost and angry."

I decided to address the spirit directly. I wanted her to acknowledge her death to prepare her for the eventual depossession. "How did you kill yourself?"

"OD'd—I swallowed aspirins. (Pause.) I don't feel well. I feel a lot of pain in my abdomen. (Long pause.) Jean swallowed aspirin too, before she jumped off the bridge. I wanted her to live. I didn't know what to do. I couldn't talk to her. I was . . . just with her. It wasn't my fault she died! (Long pause.) We'd been together—all three of us, for a long time."

I asked her to look for her loved ones, who were there to take her to the spirit world.

"Nobody's here. Jean was my only friend."

"Somebody's here for you. Look around."

"No."

I decided that continuing this tack would be futile. Knowing she was fat, I imagined she could be persuaded to leave if she felt she could have a slender body. I asked her if she wanted a body of her own that would be slim and lovely—without dieting!

"That's a stupid question!"

I noticed a big smile on her face—it was working! I told her about the Light and how, when she entered it, she would find herself in a perfect body.

"I think that's real funny. How is light going to change my body? How do you know that?"

I pointed out that there was a teacher who had come to help her understand. Also, I suggested that after she went into the Light, she undoubtedly would be with Jean.

"There are two."

"What do they say to you?"

"They want to help me, just like they did years ago. I don't know why anyone would want to help me, after all these years."

I asked her what her teachers were saying to her.

"They want to help me." Looking to the side, she seemed to address invisible beings. "What are you going to do to help me?"

Then, turning back to me, "They promise . . . I don't know if I [illegible]ld trust anybody. I want to go see Jean . . . go where she [illegible]ing.)

[illegible] they say about that?"

[illegible]ake me to her, because we are both needing the

same help. (Pause.) Now I'm walking toward the Light. It's like a spark getting bigger and bigger . . . it's *so* bright! I can't keep my eyes open. They say 'That's okay.' I've got goose bumps. It's not hot . . . but, it's good. It's not mysterious. I'm beginning to relax. My body is very light! I don't feel the body. It's not a body. It's very different . . . like thought . . . yet I can see. There's beauty . . . and colors. I'm so *light!* (Pause.) I have a sensation, like I've stepped into cold water . . . but it's so beautiful . . . and it's only the beginning. (Long pause.) I can't go any further. There's a period of adjustment. (Pause.)

"I have a message for you. It's that there is no fear. Nothing to be afraid of! (Long pause.) I can't talk much longer through Barbara. It's not good for her, I'm being told. Only a short period of time a person should do this. Barbara can't feel her body. (Pause.) The work you are doing is very good."

I felt I better bring Barbara back into control of her body. I was concerned that she may have been out of it. I was going to take the advice of the teachers!

"Barbara, come back into your body now. When you are ready, please tell me what it was like for you to be channeling Margaret."

(Long pause.) "I couldn't feel my body. I'm just beginning to now. Like my voice is here, but my body isn't. It's like a radio tuned up to a certain vibration. Now, it's tuned down to a certain vibration. If you stay up and you're not ready, you burn out! If you stay too long, sometimes you cannot come back! It was very nice. When I came back into the body, I started with the mind, then the head, brain, shoulders, arms, down the torso. Now I can feel my calves and my feet, but I still feel lighter."

I gave her suggestions to be grounded and centered and asked her how she felt.

"I feel relaxed." She shook her hands as if they had been asleep. "The other side is not that far away. In a sense, it's a state of mind, and so easy to contact." She nodded her head. "My body feels different!"

"In what way?"

"I feel like I have been floating in the water with weights on me. I didn't drown, but I was always holding myself so I wouldn't. Part of me knew I wasn't drowning. The weights are gone. Now I'm aware I have to learn to walk all over again. I haven't really lived for so many years. I was fighting, holding on, controlling . . . satisfying everybody, except myself. Like a marionette on strings."

"Who was pulling the strings?"

"Margaret comes to mind, the red hair and the white body. Jean . . . everybody but me. Before Jean and Margaret, somebody else, and before them, somebody else. *I've allowed it!* Because I've allowed myself to be influenced by so many suggestions. I want *me* to make up my mind.

"How do I know it's not all suggestions? That I'm not making all them up? Yet it's so real, when I see it . . . so many suffering souls! Everybody claws at me to help them, but who helps me? When can I get help?

"I feel alone, in a sense. Even though I'm relieved, I feel *alone*. I'm walking with my hands behind my back and my head down. My mission in life really is to walk alone and to serve. There isn't going to be any person to help me. It's like a voice from Jesus—a spirit. I really don't understand that message. I don't *want* to understand it. It doesn't make sense that no one would help me. (Pause.) It's difficult to articulate these feelings."

Before bringing her out of hypnosis, I told her that only *she* knew whether it had been reality or fantasy and that it would become clear to her when she was ready.

Once out of trance, I asked her what it had felt like to experience the two spirits, Jean and Margaret.

"Margaret was much stronger than Jean. I couldn't remember her name. Then it popped back into my mind, like she took over my body. I wasn't aware as I was talking, but I was.

"The sensation in the Light was of total weightlessness. There's a transition period on the Other Side that you need to get used to being there. When her teachers were talking to her, it was like an echo. It was not good to stay out of the body too long. If you had touched me, I couldn't have felt it. You could have put your hand right through me.

"Margaret was very angry—nippy! 'You're not going to tell me.' That really fits well with me. Switching and changing so fast—the whole personality. And later, joy, a giving over to the good, a dissolving of all the negativity into the Light.

"The other part, the message to you—only so much was told to you at this time . . . only what you are supposed to hear.

What you are doing is important. People are not quite ready—it's a slow process.

"The difference from here to there is very thin—a state of mind. One can tap into that source, but you have to be careful. You must know what you're tapping into!"

It had been an exciting and productive session. We had both learned a great deal. It was a rare experience for me because of the many interesting twists and turns our excursion had involved: a possessing entity who was possessed herself—while she lived and as a discarnate! And the description by Margaret of being in the Light—this was a first during a depossession! Many hypnotized patients carried their own regression through their deaths, the immediate after-death experience, and the journey into the Light—and beyond. But, an earthbound spirit releasing from one she had possessed and continuing to report while out of the physical body—that was unique.

As Barbara settled herself in the chair, she announced that she had felt really good all week. There were no traces of the severe depression and suicidal thoughts she had been suffering just prior to our last session. She did feel lonely, though. It was as though she had lost some good friends.

The depression had left with Jean and Margaret, but the binges persisted. She elaborated, "Someone is forcing me to eat! It's like somebody is taking my hand and making me do it. I don't want to! There's a person saying, 'Feed me!' I feel like I'm almost out of control of my own consciousness."

"Barbara, it sounds as though you're getting to the nitty-gritty. It's funny the way spirits surface. Sometimes, it seems to me that they leave in layers. Some have to go before others can.

"Apparently, Margaret wasn't responsible for all of your weight problem. She may have contributed somewhat, but since you're still eating compulsively, my hunch is that there's someone else—the one who says, 'Feed me!' Let's use hypnosis now, and see if anyone is here."

After the hypnotic induction, I questioned Barbara's subconscious mind, using finger signals. They indicated that there was one entity with her, and another trying to hide.

Making an assumption, I asked when the "feed me" entity

had joined her. Barbara replied, "She visited me at the hospital when I had the hysterectomy." Further clarification brought out that the "visitor" was a confused spirit who wandered into her room and possessed her. I did an immediate depossession, and she appeared to leave with her loved ones without any hesitation.

Suddenly shuddering, Barbara murmured, "Dorothy's here! She died of cancer a number of years ago. She's angry at me for marrying Gary. She and Gary dated before I even knew him. She feels I took him away from her. She bounces back and forth—between him and me."

It was exceedingly difficult to persuade Dorothy to go to the Light. She was caught up in a feeling of unfairness that her body had died, while Barbara was alive and healthy. She was determined to make her rival sick.

As she put it, "If I stay in her body, she'll eat herself to death, and she will die, too—like I died. Then she will know what it's like. I was so full of life! I liked to do lots of physical things like Gary. I jumped out of planes. I sailed. My life was over so fast! It wasn't fair!"

Besides her bitterness and resentment of Barbara, she was keeping herself on the earth plane because of her strong attachment to Gary. She felt she would be a much better mate for him than his wife was. She gloated, describing how much she enjoyed being with him—while she was possessing *him*. She admitted that she deliberately created turmoil between the two and was delighted that their marriage was crumbling.

I talked to Dorothy and explained that she would have a healthy, energetic body like the one she had before she got sick. She was distrustful of my promises, but finally considered leaving when she recognized her deceased grandmother and saw that she had a real body. As I was about to bless her, she had a last-minute change of heart and refused to go.

It was time for something more than I could give her! I requested the help of specialists from the spirit world. I had found them to be extremely helpful in difficult depossessions in the past.

Barbara reported, "All you needed to do was ask. That's what they say. There are five beings. They're beautiful. Light, brilliant beings! They're forming a circle. They can't get too close to her, because their vibrations are too strong. They are surrounding her, her grandmother and an old friend, Ted. Ted is here!" Barbara's face lit up with a radiant smile as she explained, "He's a friend of my mother-in-law's. Oh, he wrote such lovely poetry!"

Then remembering, she spoke to Dorothy, "I forgot. You wrote beautiful poetry too. Even though you don't know him, he came to help you—and he can. Before he died, he was an old man—very ill! It was hard for him to walk. He had to use a cane, and he could hardly see. Now, look how beautiful he is!"

Moving her head to the opposite side, she addressed Ted. "Oh, Ted! Thank you! Thank you!"

Then, explaining to me, "The five beings are sending energy and healing. They're stationed like a five-pointed star. Dorothy's getting up. She's crying. She wants me to say, 'Goodbye' to Gary." After a long pause, during which she was smiling, she continued, "That Light is *so* healing. It's such a temptation to just walk into it. But I can't!"

I asked if Dorothy had left. Wiping a tear from the corner of one eye, she nodded, and her "yes" finger lifted.

At that point, I called upon healing spirits to strengthen and repair her aura and body. While I was waiting for that work to be accomplished, I had an inspiration.

Since Barbara was an unusually visual and sensitive hypnotic subject, I decided to try an experiment with her that had worked beautifully with other equally perceptive patients.

"In your mind's eye, bring Gary here right in front of you. Now, tell me if you are able to see any spirits with him."

"His father . . . and an old man." After a pause, she added, "Now, I'm aware of two others."

I addressed them, en masse, performing an absentee depossession. I explained that their bodies were dead, that they were with Gary as possessing entities, and that their loved ones had come to help them—to take them to the next stage of their lives. I blessed them, telling them to go into the Light.

She described them leaving with their helpers, and as she did, her "yes" finger lifted again spontaneously.

Another memorable session had drawn to a close. Before she left, she remarked that she felt tired, as though she had been through a lot. Indeed, she had!

11 ✻ Case Study—Paolo

"All my problems started at fifteen—before that, I was fine! I went to Italy for one year, and everything changed for the worse. I lost my self-confidence. I lost all the self-discipline I had. I didn't study, I didn't do well. Since then, I've had lots of problems. I don't understand it. That's why I'm here." Fifty-year-old Paolo had decided to take his wife's advice and do something to reverse the continuing self-destructive patterns that were preventing him from accomplishing his goals—and were making his life miserable.

I asked him what had happened in Italy that may have caused the change.

There was nothing traumatic or at all unusual. He was sent to his native land to go to the American College, a school that held classes half in English and half in Italian. His parents undoubtedly had their own reasons for sending him to his grandparents. He was told it would be good for him to practice his Italian and get to know his family before they died.

He wondered why his behavior had changed so drastically and suddenly. He commented that before, up to that point in his life, he had applied himself in school, had done well, and had enjoyed studying since he had a broad range of interests and abilities. During his year in Italy, he lost all interest in his classes and couldn't seem to motivate himself. He had to force himself just to get by.

In Italy, for the first time in his life, he had tried to pick up a girl. He wanted sex. He didn't succeed, but the desire was strong—and persisted!

His current problem was that he was out of control a great deal of the time. He drank excessively. He ate compulsively—and constantly battled thirty extra pounds. Every evening he wrestled with the decision whether to go home to his family or to stay in a motel. If he stayed, he felt guilty. If he went, he hated the confrontations with his wife. In his business dealings, he was fearful and lacked self-confidence one day, while the next day he was full of new plans and optimism.

His relationship with Kathy, his spouse of twenty-three years, was strained to its utmost. He confided, "There are certain times of the year when I have a real strong urge to run away—spring and Christmas. We've split up several times. I just walk out—and stay away for three months or so. The last time—five years ago—we came very close to divorcing. There's got to be a reason for it. I have no idea what it is."

I questioned him about his feelings for Kathy.

He spoke of having a lot of respect for her and knowing that—in many ways—she was the perfect woman for him. He scratched his head, frowned, and said, "I love her, but we fight all the time. The major conflict is sex. I can't be aroused—she doesn't turn me on. I don't know why; she used to. She's a very attractive woman. Pretty face. Nice figure. Sometimes, I can't stand the idea of going to bed with her. The sex is so bad now that I'm afraid to try." He added that he drank to escape the anxiety of all the failed attempts and to avoid going home.

Alcohol seemed to be a bigger problem than Paolo was willing to admit. He confessed that he had even blacked out during the last year. He started using it as a crutch twenty-five years ago and since then frequented bars every evening after work. When his business occasionally faltered, he would turn to drink to boost his morale.

He was arrested a year ago for drunk driving. Somehow, the fine, driving school, and the police record motivated him to discipline himself.

It worked. He stopped drinking completely. Then he found he was able to follow a low-calorie diet. Easily dropping thirty pounds, he felt terrific and energetic. He maintained the new weight and his self-esteem soared. He started going home regularly and got along better with Kathy and his three children.

Stresses in his business were the undoing of all that he had built up during that six-month period. He started drinking again. Back came the pounds—and the hassles at home.

The problem that was the heaviest on Paolo's mind was how he was handling his business. As the owner of his town's most popular hardware store, he claimed he did exceptionally well with his customers, despite his conflicts. "One minute I'm the best! The next, I'm totally paranoid. I convince myself that I won't do well—that I'll fail. I start a project and get real excited and am sure this time it will work out. Then, an overwhelming feeling undermines all my confidence and enthusiasm. I scrap the plan and turn to booze. It happens over and over. The worst part is I *know* I have the ability to be a success."

Because I was suspicious that possession might be causing most of his problems, I questioned him about his personality when he drank.

"Any changes are upbeat! I just wander around from bar to bar. My goal is getting people to like me. When I drink, I'm the life of the party with everyone—but Kathy. I get even madder at her!"

I shared my concern that he may have one or more spirits possessing him, taking over control at times and causing the many conflicts he had outlined.

He had believed in entities all his life, as did his family. He told me that the area in which he now lived was full of bad vibrations. There had been many deaths, suicides, people becoming alcoholics—and even sightings of ghosts in the old, nearby cemetery. His daughter often rode her horse by the graveyard, and on several occasions she saw a girl spirit. When she did, both she and her horse always became "spooked."

Paolo was intrigued with the idea that spirits might have been messing up his life and consented to a depossession.

As usual, I began by making a relaxation tape for him, replete with positive suggestions for generalized well-being. I ended with sleep suggestions, for him to use nightly. He appeared to go into a beautiful trance, completely releasing all the tensions that had been so obvious minutes before.

As I was recording the depossession on the opposite side of

the tape, he started speaking, interrupting the process. The voice was considerably different from Paolo's.

He angrily announced, "I'm not going anywhere!" The voice was booming and thick-tongued, as though he were drunk.

"Who are you?"

"George. But don't tell Paolo, that asshole!"

Hoping to facilitate his leaving, I asked him if he saw anyone he knew.

"Pete's here! But he's dead! What the hell! I don't care. Good ol' Pete, my buddy," he slurred.

As we talked, it became clear that his bluster was a cover-up for fear. He became frantic at times and even burst into deep sobs, as he halfway accepted that his body had died.

When I mentioned Kathy, he became vociferous. "I can't stand that broad! All she does is nag poor Paolo, that jerk!"

I asked him if it was he who decided to go drinking and stay in the motel.

"Yeah. If I never see her again, I'd be happy. But that shit goes home when he feels bad enough. I can't stop him all the time."

Even though I had stopped the depossession per se, I was still recording our conversation and could see that it might be extremely helpful in our work.

I made no attempt to have George leave during the remainder of the session. Instead I tried to educate him about his condition and planted a few seeds regarding the good life spirits lead in the afterworld.

My main aim was to establish rapport with this rather rough and bombastic character.

After Paolo was out of hypnosis, he said, "I know that guy! That's me when I've been drinking. But it's not me!"

We set up an appointment for two days later. I suggested he share the taped conversation with his wife. I assumed it would help her to understand what she had been coping with, and he would be able to get feedback from her. He left expressing his encouragement and optimism.

"Kathy said she's talked to that spirit a lot. When I've been drinking, she says she sees him coming out in me. Not really seeing, but the way I act. It's George!"

I asked him if he had felt any anxiety driving to my office. I was concerned about George's fear.

"It was strange. Yesterday I had the strongest urge to come to see you. I don't know who wanted to be here. Then, last night I got drunk. It's been a long time since I tied one on like that! And I did feel nervous the closer I got to Saratoga."

I suggested that we immediately use hypnosis, so I could talk to George.

Dr. Fiore. Yesterday when Paolo felt a very strong urge to see me, was that you?

George. Yes.

Dr. Fiore. What did you want to see me for?

George. I just wanted to hear some more.

Dr. Fiore. I'm going to help you understand. That's what you really want, isn't it?

George. (Nods.)

Dr. Fiore. Okay. Now just relax, I'm going to show you something. (Handing him the mirror.) Just open your eyes.

Do you see this face? Just relax. Do you see my hand up here?

George. Yeah.

Dr. Fiore. Do you feel my hand?

George. Yeah.

Dr. Fiore. Feel this curly hair?

George. Yeah.

Dr. Fiore. That is Paolo's face. Do you understand? That isn't your face, is it?

George. No.

Dr. Fiore. But you can feel me touching you, right?

George. Yeah.

Dr. Fiore. There's no question that I'm touching you. But you see this other face.

George. Yeah.

Dr. Fiore. All right. That is Paolo's face, and it's a familiar face, isn't it? You've seen that face before because you've looked through his eyes before, maybe when he's been shaving or getting dressed. Now take a good look. That's Paolo.

Now, you've been with him since he was probably about fifteen years old, and he's grown up now. He's a grown man, fifty years old. And he has a nice face, but it's not your face. Just close your eyes. Just relax. Calm down, now.

That's step number one, George. You have to realize that it's you in somebody else's body. You understand, don't you?

You saw that face, but it's not your face, and you felt my hand on the head that you felt was your head and you realize it's not your head. Now, the most important thing that you can learn—that anybody can learn: that I can learn, that Paolo can learn, that anybody can learn—is that what we've been taught about death is a myth. Life does continue after death, but the body does die. Your own body died. But *you* didn't die. Do you understand that now?

George. (Nods.)

Dr. Fiore. Now you're beginning to accept the idea that you are no longer in your body—that you're in Paolo's body. Okay. Are you also accepting the idea that there's no such thing as death of a person? Only death of a body.

George. (Nods.)

Dr. Fiore. You know that you're alive because you're talking to me, aren't you? And you're hearing what I say. And you feel very alive, don't you? So you haven't died. But your body did die.

Now I'd like you to take a look at this body you're in. Open your eyes and look down at it. Look at the hands. Look at the shape. Is this your own body as you remember it?

GEORGE. (Shakes his head no.)

DR. FIORE. What was your body like? About how old were you?

GEORGE. Twenty-eight . . . straight black hair . . . I like to dance. I like all the women around me.

DR. FIORE. Well, I bet you're tired of Paolo.

GEORGE. No! I haven't found somebody else I want to stay with.

DR. FIORE. Why don't you help yourself? When you go, you can have your own body. Wouldn't that be nice for a change?

GEORGE. (Yelling.) Well, I have a body.

DR. FIORE. When you leave, you're going to get a new one.

GEORGE. Naw . . . naw, you're lying to me.

DR. FIORE. Did your mother die?

GEORGE. Uh-huh.

DR. FIORE. Now, suppose you saw your mother in her body, what would that tell you?

GEORGE. That it's not real.

DR. FIORE. What if she came over and touched you? (Pause.) Do you feel somebody touching you now?

GEORGE. No.

DR. FIORE. Do you feel someone touching your hand?

GEORGE. No! No! (Crying and looking off to the side as though at someone.)

DR. FIORE. You're being very stubborn.

GEORGE. (Seemingly addressing someone else.) Just leave me alone! (Whining.)

DR. FIORE. Don't talk to your mother that way.

GEORGE. It's not my mother, it's just . . . somebody.

DR. FIORE. I don't think so.

George. (Crying.) I'm sorry, Mama. I'll be strong. (Whispering.) I'll be strong.

Dr. Fiore. You are very strong. You're being strong by realizing your condition—that's the strongest thing you can do.

George. Hello, Mama.

Dr. Fiore. Now you can see your mother, and she's in a beautiful body, it's a perfect body, I want you to notice how real it is.

George. I can't see her, I can't see her. (Whispering.)

Dr. Fiore. She's right here with you. You *can* see her. She's in her spirit body.

George. She's *not* a spirit!

Dr. Fiore. Sure she is.

George. She's got tits.

Dr. Fiore. That's right.

George. Spirit's don't . . . Oh, I don't believe it!

Dr. Fiore. She's very real, George.

George. I see a door . . . way back.

Dr. Fiore. Do you see a Light in the door?

George. It's really bright.

Dr. Fiore. Keep looking at that Light, and tell me what you feel when you see it.

George. (Long pause.) Oh, it's pulling me.

Dr. Fiore. The minute you step into that Light, you're going to find yourself in a body. You'll be twenty-five years old, would you like that?

George. Uh-huh.

Dr. Fiore. And handsome. You'll have a body with dark hair —no gray—slim.

George. No, I don't want to go!

Dr. Fiore. You don't have to. I told you, I'm not going to make any effort to force you. If you want to go, you can give it a try. If you don't like it, Paolo will let you come back.

George. Oh, no he won't! If he gets rid of me, he'll *never* let me come back!

Dr. Fiore. Well, I'm going to ask him to let you come back. I know that when you go into that life, *no way* you'd come back here. Why would you trade a fifty-year-old body for a twenty-five-year-old one—somebody else's body for your own? I know that you are not going to want to come back. It's the last thing you're ever going to want to do, because you'll have your own body, it will be strong and healthy.

George. Shut up, Paolo!

Dr. Fiore. What's he saying to you?

George. He's after me to go. And I don't want to!

Dr. Fiore. You don't have to. You don't have to. Would you like us to just—you don't want to take me up on this deal today, right?

George. What deal?

Dr. Fiore. The deal of going and coming back—say, in a week, if you don't like it.

George. No!

Dr. Fiore. I didn't try to force you, did I?

George. You're going to try and trick me out.

Dr. Fiore. No, wait a minute. No tricking and no forcing. I want you to think about what I've said to you, that life continues after the death of the physical body.

You just happen to be stuck in somebody else's body. If you had gone into the spirit world when you should have, all of this time you would have been in a body that would never age, and it'd be perfect in every sense of the word. I want you to think about that between now and next time, okay?

GEORGE. (Pause.) Do you believe in reincarnation?

DR. FIORE. Yes. I think so. Do you?

GEORGE. *I'm afraid of it!* (Belligerent.)

DR. FIORE. Why?

GEORGE. Because what am I going to come back as? What kind of person?

DR. FIORE. You're the one that makes the decision.

GEORGE. What decision?

DR. FIORE. Well, when I work with patients in hypnosis, they remember that they got together with their guides and then decided what their next life would be like.

GEORGE. Why would someone want to come back like some of these assholes around here?

DR. FIORE. Well, you'll have a lot to say about that, and it will be a very interesting experience. Now let's talk . . .

GEORGE. (Interrupting.) I was trying to read a book about reincarnation, but I kept stopping because I didn't want to know too much about it. (Long pause.)

(Laughing.) Well, Paolo's telling me, he doesn't believe me. That I'm really here!

DR. FIORE. What does he say?

GEORGE. Well, he's telling me that he doesn't believe you. But I believe you! (Laughing.) I sure had that son of a bitch fooled. I'm going to run away and let him suffer. The rotten son of a bitch!

DR. FIORE. It can't be too much fun being in Paolo's body.

GEORGE. Sometimes.

DR. FIORE. I want you to get used to these ideas. I'm here to help you put an end to this prison that you've created for yourself . . . to help you to be in your own body.

GEORGE. (Sighing loudly.)

DR. FIORE. What's the matter?

GEORGE. I'm getting mad. I'm mad at this whole situation. Because Paolo's going to let Kathy listen to that tape, and she's going to know. And she's going to understand. She'll be mad!

DR. FIORE. Calm down.

GEORGE. And I don't like that!

DR. FIORE. Calm down, calm down. Come on.

GEORGE. She ain't gonna be like you.

DR. FIORE. Come on, calm down. You may not be around to have to face all of that. I bet you were kind of a handsome guy, weren't you? Well, you could be in that exact body again, whenever you decide to go.

GEORGE. That body?

DR. FIORE. Yes . . . and soon.

GEORGE. Oh, God! (Crying.) Oh, God!

DR. FIORE. It's not the end of the world. It's the beginning—for you. Nothing bad's happening, so calm down.

GEORGE. I don't want to be a nice guy.

DR. FIORE. That's fine, too.

GEORGE. I'm going to do it.

DR. FIORE. What are you going to do?

GEORGE. I want to be a nice person.

DR. FIORE. You really do?

GEORGE. Yes. (Crying.) I really do.

DR. FIORE. All right. Here's somebody to help you leave.

GEORGE. I don't know him. (Frantic and crying.)

DR. FIORE. Yes, you do.

GEORGE. Uncle Jim.

Dr. Fiore. What does he say to you?

George. He asked me to go. But I don't wanna go! (Crying.) They're all dead. How can I go with dead people? (Crying hard.)

Dr. Fiore. Listen to me! Listen to me! Calm yourself!

George. Awwww . . . fuck it!

Dr. Fiore. Just calm yourself. Would you like me to explain to you everything that's happened?

George. Uh-huh.

Dr. Fiore. And there's only one thing that you have to do, the simplest thing in the world. You just have to open up your mind. I know you're tough, but you like to think of yourself as open-minded, don't you? All right, now I want you to look at the evidence. I'm not going to talk you into anything. Your Uncle Jim is here, your mother is here, and Pete, your old friend, is here. All for you. And they're going to explain things to you between now and next time. Okay?

Now if you decide you want to go, you can go. You don't have to wait until Paolo comes back here. Now, if you need some extra help in going, I'll be happy to help you next time. That's what I'm here for. So I'll just say good-bye to you for now. Okay, my friend?

George. (Grunts.)

Dr. Fiore. Bye-bye. You just slip into the back now and let Paolo come back.

Paolo was pleased with the positive changes he had observed during the past week. Counting on his fingers, he listed the improvements. "The drive to eat is diminished. The drive to drink is nonexistent. Lots more positive feelings toward Kathy. I even like going home at night. More efficient in all areas."

He felt he had better control now, which he attributed to his knowledge of what was going on. He felt that the idea of possession explained a lot that was inexplicable before. Looking puzzled, he added, "I don't know if there's still somebody with me or not. My mind blanks out. I'll be concentrating on something, then I'll be doing something else, like looking over here," he pointed to the right, "and then I can't remember what I was doing!"

He recalled that the previous Friday night after finishing up at work, he had made up his mind to go home. He then had the strongest urge to stop and have a drink. Being firm in his decision not to give George what he wanted, he said aloud, "No, you don't! I'm not giving you anything!" He then drove off to take care of an errand.

After finishing—as he walked toward his car—he noticed the headlights were on. He distinctly remembered turning them off after parking the car. He explained that since two-lane roads were dangerous, he had a habit of driving with the lights on, and always turned them off automatically—he had for years. "I guess somebody thought if the battery was run down, I wouldn't be able to go home . . . It must be George. He sure hates Kathy!"

On Saturday, he tried self-hypnosis. He talked to George, who almost left—but someone walked in the room and interrupted the depossession.

At that point, I suggested that we use hypnosis.

He settled back, reclining the chair to its maximum. I covered him with the blanket. Closing his eyes and responding to my hypnotic suggestions, he quickly drifted into the sleeplike drowsiness that is characteristic of a trance state. I then turned my attention to George.

Dr. Fiore. How are you, George?

George. Fine.

Dr. Fiore. Good! How did you feel about coming here to see me today?

George. I didn't want to.

Dr. Fiore. Paolo told me you almost left the other day, but someone interrupted you.

George. Yeah. I had some pretty good people pulling on me.

Dr. Fiore. Why were they pulling?

GEORGE. Because I didn't want to go.

DR. FIORE. Are you a little nervous about going?

GEORGE. Not really.

DR. FIORE. What's troubling you?

GEORGE. I've been here such a long time. I'm so tired! Real tired!

I talked to him about the beautiful life he would have, and how he would be able to rest and be with loved ones.

GEORGE. A lot of people are holding their hands out to me.

DR. FIORE. Take someone's hand.

GEORGE. I want to, but I just can't. *Can't.* (Desperately.)

I soothed him and tried to help him recognize familiar faces among those who were there. He was too frantic.

DR. FIORE. Relax. Do you want me to hypnotize you?

GEORGE. I'm already hypnotized.

DR. FIORE. I'm going to hypnotize you some more. Listen to my voice.

I suggested that he progressively relax "his" body. He quieted down and appeared much calmer. Then I explained that leaving was the easiest thing he could do. I told him that a lovely person was putting her arms around him. Perhaps it was his mother, a sister, a girlfriend. She was holding him and would stay with him and help him, she had missed him very much.

(Long pause.) "He's gone!" Paolo blurted out.

"How do you feel?"

"Upset!" He cried, tears streaming down his face and neck. "I feel free!" Uttering a loud sigh, he exclaimed, "Oh, God! . . . that voice I always hear is gone!" Deep sobbing wracked his bulky frame. "Oh, God! Oh, I wasted *so* much time! *So* much of my life, God! I've got so much to do!"

* * *

I felt that Paolo had just cured himself of the affliction he had had all those thirty-five years. As I shared these thoughts with him, he seemed excited and radiant.

As he left, I felt joyous, sure that he had healed himself—and George—at a deep spiritual level. Time would tell.

"I couldn't believe it! Sex with Kathy was better than it's been in twenty years! I'm going home a lot. And I feel totally averse to drinking, too. But, the best thing is how great our sex life is now. That George *really* hurt me! It feels *so* good to have him gone!"

Paolo returned to my office two weeks later for his fourth therapy session. He continued, "It was a little less than a month ago I came for the first time. I'm amazed at the complete change!"

"One spirit can affect every area of your life, Paolo. He was *very* dominating—and just took over. But—remember—you had your power, too. If not, you never would have married Kathy. He wouldn't have permitted it. It's no wonder that you've had problems throughout your whole marriage. He's the one—I'm sure—who got you to leave those times. You were still responsible, though. You could have stopped him, if you really wanted to. The problem was you didn't realize you had an entity with you. You thought it was you. But that's all water under the bridge now."

He frowned and leaned forward in the chair, putting his elbows on his thighs and holding his forehead. Obviously something was troubling him.

"Nothing's changed with my attitude about success. I'd hoped that it would have. I can't make it big, thinking the way I do. I just see myself as a loser."

I commented, "Rome wasn't built in a day." Pointing out that there's a cause for any problem, I suggested that his bout with possession may not have been over yet. "It's highly unlikely for you to have just one spirit, with all the drinking you did. Each time, you opened up your aura, and others could very easily come on board. Also, it may be that there's a past life affecting you."

"Yeah. When you mentioned spirits it reminded me of what

happened yesterday. We're in the process of moving, and as I was loading my stuff from the garage, I started feeling overwhelmingly depressed. I could feel it drawing on me. When I left the house, I felt a little better. But I felt pursued all day."

Suspecting that nothing really new had happened, I asked, "Have you felt this before?"

"Yeah! But when George was with me, I felt bummed out a lot, especially at home. I didn't realize the difference until yesterday. It's strange, because I was feeling great—until I walked into the garage."

I asked him to elaborate.

"Nothing is right. Nothing is *ever* going to be right. Just a whole lot of negatives. After I left, I wondered if somebody had committed suicide in the garage. That would explain how down I felt."

I believe that we experience life at two levels—or more—simultaneously: at the conscious level and at a subconscious one—the inner mind. His subconscious mind would have been aware of discarnates and would have known a great deal about them. It certainly would have registered any impact they'd had on him.

I suggested that we check out whether he had picked up one or more earthbound entities. He agreed. When I began the hypnotic induction, his eyelids started fluttering, a sign that he was already going into trance.

After he went deeper, I asked him to go back in his memory banks to the day before—when he was in the garage.

Paolo. A lot of lights around me—moving figures. All of them are pushing down on me . . . like a heavy blanket. *Really heavy!* I just *have* to get out of here!

Dr. Fiore. Does anybody come with you?

Paolo. Somebody's just hanging onto the outside of me.

Dr. Fiore. Not inside?

Paolo. Right.

I addressed the entity who was attached to his aura, and asked if a loved one was present. The spirit answered that his wife had come. I performed a depossession, and he apparently went with her into the Light.

Paolo remarked, "I could feel some chills. When he left, it felt like a little blanket slowly being lifted." With a big sigh, he added, "A lightness."

Just to be sure, I asked who else was there. The answer was "Barry." He left with his mother. Paolo described it as, "Like someone's pulling him . . . he's gone!"

Now it was time to address the problem that worried him the most: his lack of success in business. Since he had experienced the same fear of failure since George's departure, we couldn't blame it on him.

I asked Paolo's inner mind to take him to the event responsible for that conflict.

Paolo. I keep wanting to think about the twenties. A big business man—*really* powerful. He did a lot of manipulating of people—a lot of illegal things. (Long pause.) I had a beautiful wife, but I still messed around. She left me. I started going to hell. Everything I had went to hell. I had nothing. I became a drunk on skid row . . . sitting on the street with nothing. God, I hated it! *It was awful!* Sitting there in my own spot. (Pause.) Still feel like that. I am nothing. I have nothing. I'll never go anywhere. I deserve it. (Long pause.) I see me there . . . and it's awful.

Dr. Fiore. Are you out of your body, as you watch yourself?

Paolo. Yes. I feel sorry for that person sitting there. Wish I could leave him. I want to go away someplace else . . . but I don't want to die. It didn't occur to me to kill myself. (Long pause.) I'm starting to feel better . . . standing up . . . really happy. I'm dancing around . . . at this party. (Pause.) It's real bright. I'm the only one there!

I wanted to explore the change in the person from a very successful business man to a skid-row bum, so I regressed him back from the obvious after-death experience of being in the Light to the time when he was successful.

As he progressed through that time period, it appeared that he had become possessed while drinking and associating with call girls. As he put it, "He took me unawares. Then, all I wanted to do was quit working and play." From that point on, there was the inevitable downhill slide.

Out of hypnosis, Paolo began laughing loudly—tears running down his face. At first it was hard to tell whether he was crying or laughing. Maybe it was a little of both!

"I feel *wonderful!* A big weight has been lifted off me! I already feel different. That must have been my last lifetime. I've always been attracted to the twenties . . . the clothes, the music, the lifestyle. No wonder!"

It felt as though he had achieved his therapeutic goals with that session. I told him, "The proof of the pudding is in the eating." No matter how relevant depossessions or regressions are, only his life outside the office would show what had been accomplished.

I've learned from experience that when people are relieved of their major problems, life becomes too pressing—and interesting—for them to return for a follow-up. Most of my patients don't consider themselves in an ongoing therapy. They only want resolution of their symptoms. Even when they've agreed to let me know how they've responded to the treatment, they rarely have. However, I'm convinced that at the time they intend to. Sometimes, years later, I've run into them somewhere, or a new patient they've sent to me has told me that their problems were eliminated—completely! That news was always rewarding, and I've often wondered about the ones I didn't hear from.

As we were concluding our session, I asked him to call and let me know how he was—if he felt no need to return.

So, Paolo, of course, promised he would either come back for another appointment, or let me know how our work had affected him.

Six weeks later, I called Paolo to see how he was doing.

The report was excellent. He was feeling energetic and optimistic: the desire to drink was totally gone: he was going home all the time, and his marital relationship, he estimated, had improved seventy-five percent since our first session: he had dropped eight pounds—without dieting. He was under control! Better stated, he was in charge of his own life!

When I asked him about his problems with business, his voice changed, reflecting his disappointment, "It's still a problem—but better. Not what I know I can do."

"When you want to work on it, Paolo, give me a call. It sounds now like we'll have to look into a few more past lives to see why you are blocking your success."

He agreed to call after he returned from a business trip—when some time opened up in his schedule.

I knew he'd come for help when he was ready to face himself—through previous life regressions.

12 * Spirit Entry

You learned a great deal about possession from the last five chapters, through the lives of formerly possessed people. Many questions may have been answered for you, but probably more came to mind. Undoubtedly, the most important was, "What can I do about it?" First, you need to understand what creates the vulnerability that sets the stage for possession.

We seem to be protected from possession by the strength of our auras. When they are vibrating at high frequencies, they cannot be entered by spirits vibrating at lower ones. I explain this process to my patients as follows: "Suppose that your aura is vibrating at one thousand—just an arbitrary figure—then, only energy systems of one thousand or greater can penetrate it. If its vibrations drop to five hundred, spirits vibrating at five hundred to 999, who could not have gained access before, can now enter with ease. Any situations, emotions or behaviors that lower the vibrations of your aura increase the likelihood of possession."

The aura is to the emotional-mental-spiritual dimension of a person as the immune system is to the physical body. Just as a weakened immune system leaves the individual susceptible to diseases and infections, so a diminished aura creates a vulnerability to spirit intrusion.

I have found two major categories of conditions or behaviors that have resulted in possession: those in which people actually invited spirits to enter and those in which they were not only unaware of the possession, but completely unwilling—at a conscious level—for it to happen.

Unwilling Possession

I believe we are spirits inhabiting physical vehicles—our bodies—which we shed at death, much as we discard old worn-out overcoats. The consciousness of the body comes from the inner being—the self, which is connected to the body by a "silver cord." The body becomes unconscious when the spirit leaves temporarily. It's interesting to me that our language recognizes this idea. For example, we say he "passed out" or "was knocked out." An accident, drug overdose, blow to the head, any condition that creates unconsciousness—even briefly—"opens the door" for possible possession, because the aura is extremely vulnerable at that time and when consciousness is being regained.

One of the reasons general anesthesia is effective, I feel, is because it forces the person out of the body, hence it becomes unconscious and can be operated on without pain.

Hypnotic regressions reveal that during operations patients are usually above their bodies, watching the surgery—sometimes with detached interest. Often children, emotionally and mentally the same out of their bodies as in them, feel terrified and abandoned as we saw in Howard's case in chapter 1.

When the anesthesia wears off, the bodies become habitable again, and the original spirits—the patients—reenter.

Doctors, nurses, hospital personnel, paramedics, chiropractors, undertakers and people who work in cemeteries are all targets for possession because of the nature and location of their work.

If we could see clairvoyantly, we would probably be shocked at the number of spirits that populate hospitals. People die, often drugged or in a state of confusion and fear, and may remain there, earthbound. Most—not realizing they are dead—expect the nurses and doctors to continue taking care of them—sometimes to the extent of possessing them. One entered my patient, a male nurse, while he was administering mouth-to-mouth resuscitation as the spirit's body died from a drug overdose. Other spirits are so desperate to "live" that they bulldoze their way into any victims who suit their purposes.

John was one such entity. He spoke to me through my hypnotized, alcoholic patient, Glen. He told of dying from a massive heart attack during a treadmill stress test at a local hospital. He was livid at what had happened and thought of only one thing—getting back into his body. He also desperately needed a drink! Then he spotted Glen, who had been admitted to the cardiac center for overnight observation after experiencing symptoms of a heart attack that were later diagnosed as intense indigestion. Realizing he had no means of reclaiming his own body, John deliberately glided into Glen's, and within days was drinking again. From then on, Glen regularly drank vodka, which he formerly disliked, getting drunk frequently. In chapter 6, we saw how this entity nearly killed him.

The spirits that are roaming around in hospitals easily latch onto people whose auras are open. Severe illness greatly impairs the aura, so most hospitalized patients are vulnerable. This is especially the case with young children who can be readily dominated by adult entities. However, many times their possessors are seen as comforting persons and welcomed. Once they are possessed, their auras are weakened even more, for they blend with the auras of their possessors which are generally negative, because of their fears and confusion. With diminished protection, they are now open prey for still others desiring physical bodies. The more spirits that come "on board," the lower the vibrations of the possessee's aura.

Behaviors that definitely put people in jeopardy are drug and alcohol abuse. Even innocent experimentation with "recreational" drugs has resulted in years of possession. Every one of the hundreds of patients I have treated who had abused drugs and alcohol was possessed! In *all* cases there were many entities, most former drug users themselves, who continued their habits through their victims, continually weakening them for further possession. One recovered alcoholic patient I treated still had eighteen alcoholic spirits with her, despite having been dry for four years!

Excessive negative emotions like anger, depression and grief all lower the frequency of the aura and diminish its protection temporarily. Fatigue, especially exhaustion, and illness also weaken the aura's protective capacity. If there are spirits nearby waiting for bodies to enter, they slip right in.

The deaths of loved ones or close friends create vulnerability because of the physical and emotional upheaval the survivors feel. To add to their problems, they usually have exposure to the three places in which there are the greatest concentration and number of spirits: hospitals (including nursing homes and convalescent hospitals), funeral homes and cemeteries. Often there is drinking following the funeral services. Any spirits who followed the guests and family members home can now easily possess them.

Ties of love and affection sometimes create binding attractions when the loved ones die. Often the deceased are prevented from going on and are pulled magnetically back into their survivors' auras.

I remember one such case. Grace grieved excessively after her boyfriend died: she was a sophomore in college when he was killed in a car accident. She wrote poem after poem to him and held "imaginary" conversations with him. Then she began having problems that, years later in my office, she discovered were because of his incorporation of her at that time.

Many of my patients have found that their parents were with them and had been since the parents' deaths. Paradoxically, they were often the hardest to persuade to leave. They felt they knew what was best for their children and didn't want to hear what I, a stranger, had to say about it!

In the vast majority of cases, the victims were both unwilling to be possessed and unaware of it. Some people, however, deliberately asked to be possessed—without realizing the consequences!

Willing Possession

Popular writers, including Shirley MacLaine, Jane Roberts, and Ruth Montgomery, have opened the minds of millions to the realms of the supernatural. I feel they have contributed greatly to advancing the spiritual growth of people throughout the world, who are now eager for their own psychic experiences. One of the most fascinating is learning about the afterlife and its inhabitants, so many people try to receive messages from spirits.

Because of this growing interest, the Ouija board has remained popular for decades. The game comprises a board printed with the alphabet, numbers, a "yes" and a "no"; and a planchette, a small triangular object with short legs and a pointer. Several people sit around the board, placing their fingers lightly on the planchette, posing questions for spirits to answer by *taking over* their hands. This causes the planchette to move around the board, spelling out responses. It can be interesting, exciting, fun—and devastating!

Automatic writing is another way that people extend invitations to spirits to temporarily incorporate them. The usual practice is that they hold pens or pencils on paper, waiting for entities to use their arms and hands to write messages. This can be dangerous, because it may attract spirits who do not respect other people's properties—their bodies!

A patient told me about an experience she had many years before. She was learning to write automatically from a medium and was receiving interesting communications in different handwritings. One night, she awoke to find her hand "writing" in the air. She couldn't control it, despite all her strength and will. After ten minutes of terror, it stopped suddenly. She gave up her training and never had another similar experience. She was fortunate, indeed. Her teacher continued receiving messages in foreign languages she didn't know, and also musical scores. Her writing accelerated—but her defenses crumbled and she was hospitalized!

Her experience was similar to a would-be patient I never saw. My secretary received an urgent call from a woman who frantically insisted on seeing me that same day. She was afraid she was losing her mind and was exhausted and panicky as a result of spirits forcing her to write messages night and day. She was referred to a mental health center, as I was completely booked. I've often wondered what happened to her, and I hope she got the help she needed.

Opening up to spirits doesn't necessarily lead to possession, but if it doesn't, it's a blessing—the barriers have been lowered—voluntarily!

People lament, "I only wanted highly evolved spirits to come through—good ones." "I didn't expect this!" With a carte blanche invitation, *any* kind of spirit can come in and stay.

The Exorcist, a movie about a demonically possessed girl, was based on an actual case of a boy whose diabolical possession resulted from playing with a Ouija board. In the movie, a Catholic priest, a trained and experienced exorcist, was killed during the exorcism. Many exorcists have lost their lives during or subsequent to an exorcism!

Now that you're aware of the ultimate in consequences—demonic possession—I'll show you less catastrophic results. Fortunately, in Tina's case, the entities were earthbound, but even so, they almost caused permanent insanity.

Tina came to see me because her mother "sent her." Early, in our one and only session, she made it clear she didn't think she needed my help. As she put it, "I don't hear the voices any more."

A short, overweight, highly sensitive young woman in her early twenties, she came dressed entirely in black—stockings and all. She told her story, beginning with a nervous breakdown that had occurred two years earlier. Suddenly, after an intense period of using a Ouija board, Tarot cards, and doing automatic writing, she began hearing voices in her head. They identified themselves as the same three who had been giving her messages through the board and her writing. "They were real nice, polite and friendly. They talked a lot—all day long."

Tina explained that she would ask them questions about school and her friends, and they would give her answers and advice. When I asked if they had been helpful, she hedged and continued, "They were my friends. They even said 'Good night' and stopped talking so I could sleep." She elaborated upon her friendship with them, and then, frowning, said, "Then they got mean and said bad things like 'nigger' and 'you're a murderess.' " She noticed that the voices were different and surmised that her original friends had gone.

The voices became so persistent she couldn't carry on a conversation with other people and finally, exhausted and confused, had to drop out of college. She told the new "batch" to leave—but that made them berate her even more. By now she had a great many physical symptoms, the worst being intense vomiting that lasted for twenty days. Her worried parents took her to a psychiatrist who diagnosed her as schizophrenic, started therapy and medication, and arranged for her to spend her days in a special unit at a mental health center, returning to her home at night. After a year—still on medication—she was able to return to college on a very limited basis, taking only one simple course, like singing.

Ending her history, she added that she couldn't understand why her parents took her Ouija board away. Even after I explained what I thought had happened to her—possession—she quietly and firmly stated that she had no intention of giving up her automatic writing, because she was still "having fun" with the three original spirits—her friends, who had returned.

Since she was seeing her psychiatrist regularly, she didn't want to continue our treatments. I felt the real reason was that she knew I felt that both she and her "friends" would be better off if they went into the spirit world where they belonged.

Another practice that deliberately opens the door is "sitting" in a seance. Here, the idea is for a group of people to contact spirits. Often these people have no idea how the entities will manifest. I've heard of teenagers who—playing around half seriously—were terribly frightened when something did happen. Again, like the Ouija board and automatic writing, the call goes out to spirits. If there are particularly sensitive psychic people or any with weakened auras, they may be incorporated—and not temporarily.

We have seen a number of ways—the Ouija board, automatic writing and seances—in which people have deliberately allowed spirits to enter. And we saw earlier how some were unwillingly possessed. These are two broad categories. Many times the boundaries are fuzzy. In the "border" between the two is an area in which people reach out to spirits for help or to overcome loneliness or loss. They open themselves, wanting contact, in an unplanned way. Sometimes they get much more than they bargained for.

An amusing example comes to mind. In the beginning of her treatment, Marilyn released a few entities: her dominating mother and other relatives. In a later session, she sheepishly confessed she had been wrestling with an important decision and had called upon spirits to help her, even though she was aware of the potential dangers. She laughed and said, "So many chimed in with their opinions—I had a committee—all disagreeing with each other!'' We discovered that a few had stayed with her, as she had suspected.

A phenomenon that is not generally understood is the invisible or imaginary playmate. Under hypnosis, it's been clear to my patients that these were actually spirits. Close bonds of friendship and a mutual dependency at one point resulted in a merging of the two, the spirit and the child. From then on, they cohabited the body and the possessed was consciously unaware of the possession.

I believe that most of my patients who were possessed by many spirits, and who frequently picked up new ones in between therapy sessions, were ''uncontrolled'' mediums or ''sensitives.'' This was especially the case when they had *not* abused drugs and alcohol. The slightest things weakened their auras: eating a meal with MSG or taking one tablet of pain medication. Even driving by a cemetery or visiting a friend in the hospital resulted in a new possession.

I feel that one of the reasons some people are more psychic than others is because they have an ability to tap into their own subconscious minds that most do not have. Further, I believe that we are all subconsciously aware of each other's subconscious minds, but that what we pick up from them does not generally ''percolate'' up to our conscious minds, where we could use the data. Sometimes, when it does break through, we have a ''hunch,'' a premonition or intuition about something.

Psychics have a special rapport with their inner minds. Unfortunately, this sensitivity is a double-edged sword, for it appears from my treatment of them that they are particularly vulnerable to possession. It seems some have weakened barriers—defenses—between their conscious and subconscious minds. This allows negativity (fears, traumatic memories, etc.) from the subconscious to surface, resulting in emotional instability, which of course lowers the frequency of their auras. This, coupled with their desire to help people, even spirits, results in possession, which usually began in childhood. This is especially the case with clairvoyants who saw spirits as children.

A few of my patients—interested in metaphysics—relentlessly pursued their development as mediums and psychics, despite my advice, and were constantly picking up new spirits. We released them, and I tried to reduce their inner negativity as much as possible in order to strengthen the integrity of their auras. It was like trying to plug up holes in a dam.

From my conversations with *trained* mediums in Brazil and England, I've learned that they too have had these experiences, much to their own discomfort and their families', until they brought their mediumship under control. Sometimes this involved intense training and help from other mediums for a few years. Then, they used their sensitivity in a reasonable and beneficial way—to serve others. Unfortunately, in this country we have few, if any, centers where people can receive this kind of training. I see my therapeutic role with these people as stopping the mediumship—except in rare cases—and helping the person become more grounded, centered and balanced.

Earlier I compared the aura to the immune system—they both protect us. I have shown you how people lower the vibrations of their auras willingly and unwillingly, with possession as the result. Now I want to share with you a puzzling finding that raises many more questions than it answers.

A number of my patients have traced the origins of their possessions back to their births, childhoods or adulthoods, when they were happy and well. They just "picked up" spirits. They didn't do anything to create a vulnerability. I could find no reason for it—yet they *were* possessed.

In keeping with the analogy of the immune system, perhaps some people have an inherent susceptibility, comparable to a genetic weakness in the physical body.

Perhaps the explanation lies in past lives. Maybe possession was their karma. It could be that there were bonds formed between the possessees and the possessors during former lifetimes. In many complicated cases of possession, especially if the possession did not succumb to all my strategies, I've found that there were past-life connections and motivations for the possession. In the case of Anne, you saw the strong bond between her and her possessor, the result of a love affair in a past life.

Now that you have seen how spirits gain entry into the auras and bodies of people, let's look at a more positive aspect—how you can start to do something about possession by detecting it. Once the diagnosis is made or suspected, steps can be taken to eliminate the condition. The next two chapters will show you techniques for accomplishing these goals.

13 * Detecting Spirit Possession

Now that you have seen from the case studies how five people experienced their possessions, you may have noticed certain symptoms that many had in common, as well as some symptoms that were unique to each particular case. In chapter 6 I also showed you the various ways possession affects people.

In order to help you assess whether you are or someone you are concerned about is possessed, I'll describe the signs and symptoms that are the clearest indicators. Remember, it's generally the overall effect that is important, not one or two symptoms.

1. The one characteristic that every possessed person experiences is a persistent lowered energy level. One particularly good time to check your energy is in the morning. Lie quietly in your bed—just before getting up—and tune into your body. Check whether you feel ready for the day and have enough energy to take care of your needs. *Use your common sense!* There can be many reasons for tiredness: poor quality or insufficient sleep, your activities of the night before, allergies, crises you may be struggling with, and stress. All things being equal, if there are no logical reasons for your fatigue, consider it a positive sign of *possible* possession.

2. The most revealing characteristic of possession is changes in your personality—sometimes rapid mood swings. For exam-

ple, do you occasionally use language or act in ways that are out of character? Do you think "that's just not me"? This may happen especially if you have had too much to drink or have been under the influence of drugs. Have people told you that at times you are like "another person"?

Have you noticed a sudden change in yourself? If it happened after the death of loved ones or close friends, perhaps they have joined you. Notice whether you exhibit any of their habits, interests, idiosyncrasies or personality traits. Did you call them to you or hang on to them? Did the change seem to occur after surgery or during or after a hospitalization?

3. Many of us speak to ourselves—verbally or mentally. It can be comforting and even fun. These "conversations" may have become so habitual that you are unaware of them.

When these dialogues are between you and an entity, they can disclose a lot about your possessor's personality and your "relationship": who's afraid or angry, and who's the boss.

When you tune into the thoughts of the entity and accept them as your own, it is hard to differentiate whose they are.

Many of my patients have later realized that when they thought they were talking to themselves, they were really talking to their possessing spirits, *whom they knew subconsciously!* Typical remarks were: "You have nothing to be afraid of." "Calm down!" "Stop it!" "You shouldn't feel that way, you have a lot to contribute." Often they spoke to "themselves" as they would to children, or other people with different personalities from theirs.

It becomes easier if the spirit "addresses" you or "talks" to you in the second person. For example: "You want to eat ice cream," or "You don't believe in spirits," etc. It is much clearer—in this case—to discern that it's not you.

Sometimes the possessors will give you commands, orders, or even berate you. Depending on the personalities of the spirits, their treatment of you may be protective, critical or demeaning: "You don't have to work so hard." "Don't let him take advantage of you." "You bitch, no one will ever love you!" "You fat slob!"

In most cases these conversations or remarks are thoughts. In extreme cases, patients have reported actually hearing voices in their heads—occasionally someone they recognized.

4. As you have seen throughout *The Unquiet Dead,* substance abuse is often a big element in possession. If you abuse drugs and/or alcohol, you can be sure you are possessed. Do you decide to give up drugs, alcohol or tobacco, and then reverse "yourself" or hear inner conversations being discussed, as above? If so, you probably have one or more spirits with vested interests in your continuing these habits.

5. Are you impulsive and do things without thinking? Perhaps you are careful about your budget, yet you go on extravagant shopping sprees. It may be others indulging themselves. Spirits have minds of their own, and they don't have to pay the consequences—or the bills!

6. If there are two or more people inhabiting your body, you may forget things and have breaks in your consciousness. This can be extremely serious; hours, or even days, can seem to be missing from your memory! Do you walk into a room and not remember why you are there? If you have a lot on your mind, it could account for this kind of behavior, but not the forgetting of whole hours, days or recent activities. If you find this happening, it's a positive sign.

7. Problems with concentration are closely related to memory loss. Is it hard for you to stay with mental activities? Is it impossible to focus your attention on what you're reading, or on conversations? Do you feel like you're in a fog at times? Perhaps you have a drugged entity or an elderly spirit with you.

8. Do you experience anxiety or depression for no discernible reason? Does it come from "out of the blue," or is it there in the background most of the time? As explained in chapter 6, that's how some spirits feel, and they are manifesting through you.

9. Spirits picked up in a hospital may have died sick, drugged and in pain, or their bodies may have been brought there after death from accidents or heart attacks.

Did you have a particularly hard time recuperating? Have you felt new pains or symptoms since your hospitalization that don't seem related to your condition? Again, use your judgment and don't jump to conclusions!

10. Your reactions to this book itself can be extremely diagnostic. If you found it hard to read, could not finish certain cases or sections because of anxiety or any other emotional response, then you probably are resonating to possessing spirits.

While they are fresh in your mind, jot down your responses and what triggered them in a notebook. You have to be your own detective, so be alert for clues! Record any behavior that seems suspicious to you. Read *The Unquiet Dead* again with your notepad close by and observe your reactions. Tune into your body's responses: heart pounding, sweating, problems breathing, trembling, tingling. These are signs of anxiety. Are there any feelings of fear or panic? Become very aware of yourself.

Now that you have read through the ten most common signs of possession, it's time for you to evaluate yourself or someone you are concerned about.

It helps to be as objective as possible. Do you have people in your life with whom you feel comfortable sharing your concerns? If so, ask them to assess you on the checklist that follows and discuss any additional evidence they may have noticed.

Checklist of Possession

The following items have been put together from the material above to create a checklist for assessing the possibility of possession in yourself or others. Since most items on the list could be the result of other conditions, don't assume that you have "visitors" because of just one or two items. It's the overall picture that's important. The advantage of a checklist is that it will help you become more discerning, and this finely tuned discrimination can lead to an awareness of possession. Once you know or suspect the cause of your condition, you can begin to do something to help yourself and your possessor.

Scores

No problem, not noticed—0
Sometimes, not a big problem—1
Always now, most of the time, or yes—2

Checklist

1. Low energy level
2. Character shifts or mood swings
3. Inner voice(s) speaking to you
4. Abuse of drugs, including alcohol
5. Impulsive behavior
6. Memory problems
7. Poor concentration
8. Sudden onset of anxiety or depression
9. Sudden onset of physical problems with no obvious cause
10. Emotional and/or physical reactions to reading *The Unquiet Dead*

An overall score of 10 or more suggests possession. (A score of 2 on items 2, 3, 4 or 10 *strongly* suggests it!) If you obtained a score of less than 10, use your judgment; it does not mean that you are definitely not possessed. Just "hearing" inner voices itself could indicate that you have spirits with you.

Possession is not a "death sentence" or terminal disease. It is a condition that usually can be remedied. If you are unable to solve the problem yourself, you are still much better off than you were, because you now understand your symptoms—and you can get help. The techniques for both self-depossession and depossession of someone else will be described in chapter 14. I have included a transcript of the actual generalized depossession I use with my patients to make it easier for you, and I'll give you further advice about this in the next chapter.

14 * How to Do a Depossession

It is possible for you to free yourself or another of possessing spirits by using the technique in this chapter. Many of my patients have done so on their own between therapy sessions.

No harm can result from a depossession. At best, the entities will leave, and the worst that can happen is that they may be somewhat upset for a while and continue to stay. The depossession does not attract any new discarnates seeking "residence" in fact, it has the opposite effect—it repells them.

It is essential to be aware of certain key points when doing a depossession for yourself or someone else. The possessing spirits are lost souls, literally and figuratively. Remember that they are suffering, even if they argue that they are not. I consider them to be the actual patients, not the people who are harboring them. Rather than thinking of this procedure as "getting rid of" or "kicking out" the entities, think of it as a method of helping them in the greatest possible way. They go from totally hopeless and lost conditions to ones in which they can finally be at peace, leaving behind all their worldly concerns and fears. The main effort should be calculated to convince them of this truth. Once this is accomplished, helping them to leave becomes a simple process.

I explain to my patients that if I would forcibly remove the possessing spirits from them without assurance that they were being guided into the higher realms, I would be creating a orrendous problem for these entities and most likely for other ving people whom they would later latch onto. It is unlikely iat their new possessees would seek qualified help, and there- ore they could be saddled with their possessions for the rest of ieir lives.

The most important attitude to have during a depossession is oncern for the possessors. This is extremely difficult when there s a great toll being taken. In cases of imminent suicide, it is specially tempting to forget whose needs come first. The help f a mental health professional is a *must* in these cases and also nes involving physical violence. If the therapist is not willing to eat the condition as possession, then your own work with the pirits can continue concurrently with the professional help you re getting. Of course, the ideal situation would be one in which our therapist would help you with the entities, in which case ou'd be wise to leave the depossession entirely in his or her ble hands.

Usually you will be unaware of the identities of the possessing pirits. However, sometimes it's very clear who is with you. his is especially true if they are loved ones: parents, grandpar- nts, spouses, children or close friends.

With loved ones, it is necessary that you make a prior *firm* ommitment to let go of them emotionally. Sometimes the factor hat allowed the possession to occur in the first place was your wn emotional dependence upon them, which may have contin- ied after their deaths.

Some people have actually begged their deceased loved ones o stay with them. Patients have proudly asserted to me that they iave had their parents or spouses with them for years. They have ecounted the many ways the possessors helped them and were a onstant source of comfort and support. However, because the oved ones were earthbound spirits, both were making a tremen- lous mistake.

Occasionally, there are some minor benefits from the posses- ion, special abilities of the spirits, companionship, etc., but it is *ever* a healthy solution and prevents the spiritual growth of both articipants. It should not continue once the person who is ossessed is made aware of the situation, *no matter how close he ties!*

Depossession Instructions

The most effective way to do a depossession is to record it, using the transcript that follows or composing your own, based on the principles I'll elaborate shortly.

Playing the tape one or more times a day if necessary educates the possessing spirits repeatedly, and calls their attention to their loved ones, who will have stayed with them since the first depossession when they were called upon. Sometimes it takes a while for entities to really hear what is being said—to face their conditions and their options.

Playing the tape also gives you or the person you are helping an opportunity to notice clues that may confirm the diagnosis of possession, for sometimes spirits "hide." *Any* reactions, other than neutral interest, suggest the presence of possessing spirits. The reactions to watch for are thoughts that come to mind, such as "I don't want to hear any more," "I don't want to listen to the tape," or even more revealing, "*You* don't want to listen to it!"

Emotional responses during the depossession, such as anxiety, fear, relief, joy and anger, are those of the entity reacting.

Physical sensations are very hard for the spirit to hide: nausea, trembling and pains are excellent clues.

Keeping a journal with dates and impressions can give you an idea of when the entity leaves. If, for example, you feel nauseated four times in a row, and then do not experience it, it could be that the spirit is gone.

Another excellent way to do the depossession is to have someone—spouse, parent or friend—read the transcript to you. Or, if you are doing the depossession on someone else, read it to him or her. If you prefer, you can say it in your own words. This is particularly appropriate if you know who the possessors are, especially if they are family members.

You may get a group of people together for the purpose of helping yourself or the person you suspect is possessed. One acts as the depossessor, the others send energy to the body of the possessed by facing their palms toward his or her body, and by placing their hands very near but not touching the body. Pray together first and ask for help in convincing the entity to leave.

Each one of you should surround yourself with White Light. (Visualize a brilliant white light around you.)

If you are doing a depossession for someone else, have the possessed person relax, close his eyes, and imagine himself surrounded with White Light (see chapter 15). Then mutually ask for spiritual help and/or say a prayer. Speak directly to the entity, making the same points as described below. If you know who the spirit is, address him by name. Otherwise speak to him in general terms or read the transcript that follows.

If you believe the spirit is someone who only understands another language, speak to him or her in that language.

When you know the people and the circumstances of their deaths, it is much easier to help them. You can more readily convince them of their conditions by explaining how they died. Then, if they are loved ones, appeal to their love for you in order to persuade them to depart, explaining that their presence is harming you greatly. Reassure them that when people love each other they are never separated, even by death, and you will be "only a thought away" after they leave. Make it clear that they may return from the spirit world to visit you. Once convinced that they are indeed hurting you, and that you will not be separated forever, such possessing spirits will usually leave immediately.

If need be, in order to convince the possessors they are *not* the possessed, you may use a mirror and have them look at it and see the face of the possessed. You can point out how different it is from their own.

To help the entities overcome the most common fear—hell—tell them that a specialist in religious education from the spirit world is here to help them: priest, nun, minister, rabbi, etc.

If you suspect the spirit was sick and/or old, suggest that in the spirit world they will be able to sleep between comfortable sheets and wake up in a hospital or place where kind nurses and doctors will take care of them.

If the spirits are suspected alcoholics, drug users or heavy smokers, tell them they can have all the alcohol, drugs, cigarettes they need in the spirit world. You can point out that their loved ones are even showing them these substances. From regressions I have done it appears that, in the spirit world, entities are given these drugs and then tapered off by spirit healers and doctors at their own rate.

In problems of addiction, it is extremely helpful for the possessee to abstain from whatever substance the entity is addicted to. The going may get quite rough for a few days. This will help to show the spirit that he is more likely to get what he wants in the spirit world. One entity who had possessed a patient for forty years left because he believed the patient when he said he'd never touch another drop of alcohol again.

A frequent fear of possessing entities is that they will not exist if they leave their possessees. It is imperative to convince them that that is not true. Point out that their deceased loved ones are very alive. Have them take their hands to feel how real they are. Use your ingenuity. But convince them that their lives will continue!

You can call on whatever spirits you need for extra help. For example, a rebellious male teenager might go if the spirit of a pretty girl came for him. If a spirit comes that the possessing spirit doesn't like, call another. One male spirit detested his wife. When he saw her, he refused to leave with her. I simply called his attention to someone else, and he left readily. You can ask for spirit doctors or nurses to give sedation or tranquilizing shots. You can ask Saint Michael, Gabriel or Jesus to come.

General Instructions

1. Do the depossession at a time when you will not be interrupted. Allow a half hour, although in most cases this much time is not necessary. Try to be as well rested and as calm as possible. There should be no use of drugs, including alcohol, prior to the depossession.

2. Begin by relaxing for a few minutes in a comfortable chair or couch. Close your eyes and take three or four slow, deep breaths, inhaling and exhaling comfortably through your nose. Recite your favorite prayers—the Lord's Prayer is particularly helpful. If you have faith in certain religious figures, such as Jesus Christ, Buddha, angels, etc., call upon them to aid you with this procedure. If you are metaphysically oriented, call

upon spirit healers for aid. All this can be done mentally or verbally. However, you may find that it is easier if you speak out loud.

3. In order to protect yourself from any possible negative forces or entities, it is important to form a defensive spiritual barrier. Use the White Light technique (see chapter 15). Do this by imagining that you have a miniature sun in your solar plexus (a circular area slightly above and below your navel). Imagine that this sun is radiating a brilliant White Light, completely surrounding you with a dazzling aura that extends about an arm's length outward from all parts of your body, including your head and feet. Impress upon your mind that this aura protects you totally from any negativity or harm.

4. Address the possessing spirit, either mentally or out loud, whichever feels more comfortable, in a kindly and loving manner. If you know him, call him by name and explain that you are now aware that he is with you.

Impress upon him that he is a spirit, cohabiting your body since his own body died, and remind him of the circumstances of his death. Tell him that we are all spirits and never die—that only the physical body dies. Explain that upon his physical death he found himself outside his body, completely conscious, at which time he should have gone directly into the spirit world, where his loved ones were waiting for him. Instead, he joined you. State that, without realizing it, he has been harming you by draining your energy and confusing you, since you cannot tell his thoughts and emotions from your own.

At this point, direct his attention to his own spirit loved ones who have come to take him home to live with them. If you suspect that a certain person (his mother, his wife, etc.) is there, tell him to look for her. Instruct him to take his "escort's" hand and urge him to go with her. Explain that he has a wonderful life ahead, that he will be in a perfect body, and that it is important to you and him that he go, *now*. Tell him that hell does not exist, and that there are teachers from the spirit world to advise him about this.

Bless him as he leaves, sending him off with your love. I often make the sign of the cross, saying, "Go now in the name of the Father, and the Son, Jesus Christ, and the Holy Spirit; go in peace, light and love with my blessings." You may want to hold a cross in your right hand, or simply hold your right hand in the air, move it downward and then to the left and cross the imaginary vertical line to the right. Non-Christians may say any prayer or affirmation that is appropriate.

5. Continue to relax. Thank your spiritual helpers and spend a few minutes in a calm state.

Summary of General Points to Make

1. You are not (possessed's name).
2. Your body is dead.
3. You joined (possessed's name).
4. You are harming yourself and (possessed's name).
5. Your loved ones are here.
6. You will be in a perfect body.
7. There is no such thing as hell.
8. You will have a wonderful, peaceful life.
9. Go in peace with my blessings.

Transcript

The following is a verbatim transcript of a typical depossession that I use in my office. Sometimes I vary it depending on what I know about the entity. I'll describe these changes later in this chapter. In order to illustrate, I've used an arbitrary name, Mary. Substitute the possessed's name, or your own.

Read slowly, pausing frequently.

Depossession Technique

You're here with Mary, but you're not Mary, are you? You're somebody else completely different from her. You have a different name, different personality, different needs and ideas and attitudes. And there was a time when you were living in your own body, long before you joined Mary. (Pause.) See if you can remember back to that time. Think of a pleasant event while in your *own* body. (Long pause.)

And then something happened to that body and it died. (Pause.) When your body died you found yourself alive, just as you had been moments before, but outside of your dead body. At that moment you should have gone directly into the spirit world. Helpers were there, loved ones who came from the spirit world to escort you into your new life.

But, instead, you remained in the physical world without your own physical body. (Pause) Perhaps you were confused and didn't realize that your body had died, and therefore you didn't understand what was happening to you. (Pause.) That's where you made a *very serious* mistake, because at that moment you became a lost soul. (Long pause.)

Do you remember that you tried to talk with people and they didn't answer? Or if you touched them, they didn't seem to notice your touch? And they seemed to look right through you, as though they didn't even know you were there? Perhaps you felt very confused—upset and lonely—and frustrated, and maybe even angry with them.

The reason they didn't respond to you is because you are an invisible spirit. You weren't in a body, and so they couldn't see you. They didn't know that you were there. It's not that they were ignoring you, they just didn't realize that you were there. (Long pause.)

And then at one point you joined Mary, and that's where you made an even worse mistake. Because, you see, up until that point you had just been hurting yourself, by keeping yourself from the wonderful life you could have been having in the spirit world with your loved ones and having all of your needs met. But when you joined Mary, you started hurting her. The very least that you've done is to use her energy, causing her to be tired. And you may confuse her, because she can't tell your thoughts and wishes and needs from her own.

Now you wouldn't want someone doing this to you. Perhaps you didn't realize that you were harming Mary.

Fortunately, we can solve your problem right now, because there are people you love very, very much who have come from the spirit world to help you today. (Pause.) These are people you thought you'd never see again when they died, and here they are looking absolutely wonderful

. . . looking even better than the last time you saw them . . . with great big smiles on their faces.

They're so happy to see you, because they have been really worried about you. They've been looking for you, and searching for you, and longing for you, and now they've found you, and they're overjoyed to see you. (Pause.) And they're reaching their arms out for you. (Pause.) And now they're embracing you and giving you a warm, wonderful hug. They're holding you. Notice how wonderful that feels. (Long pause.)

Now they're holding your hand. (Pause.) I want you to notice how very real and solid their hands are. If you give them a little squeeze, you can even feel the bones underneath the skin. That's because they're in their spirit body. The spirit body is just as real and as solid as a physical body. (Long pause.)

In a few moments you're going to leave Mary, and when you do, you're going to find yourself in your very own spirit body. (Pause.) This is your rightful body, to use as long as you need to. (Pause.) And it's a perfect body in every sense of the word. It's a youthful and attractive body—a body that will never age, get wrinkles or be sick or have anything wrong with it. If you're a male, you'll find yourself in a male body, strong and healthy. If you're female, you'll be in a lovely, healthy, youthful female body. (Long pause.)

Now, just in case you are afraid of going to hell, I want you to know that there's somebody here from the spirit world—a teacher of religious education—who's going to explain to you that there is nothing to fear, because there's no such thing as hell. If you were brought up as a Catholic, this teacher-spirit is a nun or a priest. If you're a Protestant, it's a minister of your own denomination. If you're a Jew, this being is a rabbi. Whoever you need is here to explain to you that you have absolutely nothing to fear! (Long pause.)

And now it's time for you to go on to your wonderful new life. Holding the hand of your loved one and, if you like, taking the arm of your helper, know that in a very few moments, you're going to be in that Light over there. (Pause.) Perhaps you can see it in the distance, or maybe it's coming close to you. It's only seconds away. And you're going into it, hand in hand with your loved one. And the second that you do, you will be in your new, perfect body. When you go into that Light you're going to experience something that is beyond words, it's so beautiful and lovely. It's indescribably wonderful. You're going to feel completely loved and accepted. (Long pause.) You have a beautiful life waiting for you. You will be with lots of loved ones, family and friends. You're not going to be alone anymore. The worst is over. You are all right now—the best is yet to come.

(Long pause.) Now it's time for you to go. I'm asking Mary to mentally forgive you for any harm that you've done to her. (Pause.) And now go with our blessings and our love, and go in the name of the Father, and the Son, Jesus Christ, and the Holy Ghost, going in peace, and light and love. (Make the sign of the cross in the air.) Non-Christians may say any prayer or affirmation that is appropriate.

During the process, you or the person you are helping may experience a variety of intense emotions, including grief, anger or fear, but when the possessing spirit finally leaves, there is almost always a deep sense of well-being. Sometimes the person's tense body relaxes, with a sigh of relief and a big smile of joy. When you see this happening or when you feel this happening to you, you can be reasonably sure that a successful depossession has taken place.

Many people reported a feeling of "something lifting" up out of them, usually through the head, rippling up through the body or leaving through the chest or other areas. Some can actually "see" the spirits leave hand in hand with spirit loved ones, going toward a brilliant White Light. Sometimes there is no clear-cut feeling of the entities departing, but rather an awareness that they did—the person feeling lighter, relieved or changed in a positive way. Most claim to just "know" that they are finally freed of the possession. In other cases, there are no indications at the time that the spirit left, but the change afterward is remarkable.

After the depossession has been accomplished, it is important to dismiss the spirits from your mind as much as possible for the next several days. It is possible, by dwelling upon them, to pull them back to you, if they have not gone completely into the

Light. Anytime you think of them, bless them, and reinforce to yourself that they are gone, them deliberately think of something else. This is important when the spirits were people you loved deeply. I have seen cases, especially involving deceased family members, when formerly possessed people inadvertently attracted the spirits back.

The chances of your depossession working depend on how willing the entity is to leave. In *most* cases, it will be successful immediately, no matter how long the possession has lasted.

Often it may take many repeated depossessions to get the spirit, either a loved one or a stranger, to leave.

Sometimes the depossession is partially successful—the spirit leaves but does not go into the spirit world or into the Light. He or she just slips out of the body and the aura and stays with the formerly possessed person or roams around the area—only to return later. Then, another depossession is called for, with a heavy emphasis on connecting the spirit with his or her loved ones.

In such cases, it is necessary to point out to the spirits that they are still in the physical world, that they didn't go where and with whom they should have gone, and that's what caused the problem. Sometimes the entity comes back badly frightened after one of these forays! I have found, when this occurs, that they are often amenable to leaving at this point.

One particularly fascinating case illustrates this phenomenon: I think of it as a "last chance" syndrome, you will see why.

Roger came to me because of extreme feelings of inadequacy, an inability to make his life work for him. He had a very real and persistent problem, a compulsion to frequent prostitutes in local "massage" parlors on an at-least-daily basis!

After one session, we isolated the cause: a spirit named Bill, who was obsessed by sex. A depossession was performed and he left with his wife who came for him from the spirit world.

Roger looked crestfallen at our next meeting, which was on a Tuesday morning. "I had five and one half days of freedom. I didn't have the slightest desire to see a prostitute. I couldn't believe it! Went away for the weekend with my girlfriend. Sex was fine—and normal, only twice. But after dropping her off Sunday night, it hit me like a ton of bricks! I went straight over to the closest massage parlor. Since Sunday, I've had fourteen orgasms, with prostitutes and by masturbating. It's worse than ever! It [the depossession] didn't work."

I reassured him that it had worked, but not completely, that "our friend," Bill, must have come back. Sure enough, under hypnosis, Bill sheepishly confessed to slipping away from his wife deliberately, because he didn't think he would ever have sex again. He told of walking around San Jose, wondering what to do. He made up his mind to rejoin Roger and have one last fling, since he suspected I would talk him into going for good the next time! So he did. (That's why I call it the "last chance" syndrome—I've seen spirit smokers, drinkers and foodaholics all overdo because they knew they were going soon.)

Bill did leave willingly with his wife when she told him she wanted to make love with him, saying, "Quality is more important than quantity."

One trump card I reserve for *last* is to guarantee that the possessing spirits may return from the White Light if they wish. I stress that they need to go into the Light, and that they can consider it as a vacation—with a round-trip ticket that they can use. I stress that they can try it out for ten minutes, if they like, and come back. I get the patient's permission as I'm doing this. It often is the very thing that they—the possessors—need to overcome their fear of going. I use this infrequently—and it works! If they do return, I convince them that they did *not* go into the White Light—and to try again, since they know now that they may return. The second time is about one hundred percent effective.

Sometimes, one will remain, hiding. It often is a parent or grandparent: a family member who feels he is a special case. In these instances, I address and work with these spirits directly, and they eventually leave with their spirit loved ones.

Particularly stubborn entities may require the help of a professional. This is a situation in which a medium or a metaphysical minister can be of great help. Or if your own minister or priest is knowledgeable and willing to assist you, he or she can be an enormous help, because the spirit may respond to his or her authority as a man or woman of God.

Throughout the depossession process, it is very important to act as if you take it seriously—even if you don't believe it, act as if you do. Later, when it is completed, you can be as skeptical or as analytical as you want. But, during the procedure, even if you are not convinced that you or the person you are depossessing has an entity, carry through with the procedure purposefully. There can be no harm in it and, regardless of your opinion, possessing spirits may very well leave.

Never take on someone else's possessing entities in order to relieve them of their burdens—as a self-sacrifice, because you will indeed be sacrificing yourself—and the possession could last all your life! You can help without harming yourself. If you can't help, *get professional* help for the possession.

Please remember that even I, after thousands of depossessions, am still not one hundred percent convinced of the existence of spirits. But it *works!*

15* Protecting Yourself from Entities

I'm sure the question of how to protect yourself from possession has come to mind—perhaps from the beginning of this book.

Fortunately there's a lot you can do to prevent spirits from joining you. You saw in chapter 14 how to solve the problem once you are aware of it. Now I'm going to give you some pointers on how to avoid possession.

Possession can be compared to a physical illness like the flu. There are always people who never get it, despite the fact that everyone around them is coming down with it. Their immune systems are strong enough to prevent the virus from gaining a foothold.

In chapter 12, I hypothesized that the aura is to the spiritual body as the immune system is to the physical body. The *key* to protection from spirit intrusion is keeping the aura "strong." Just as there are viruses everywhere, so our world appears to be populated by discarnates as well as living human beings. The former can be denied entrance by keeping the aura vibrating at a rapid frequency.

Certain gifted people, clairvoyants, are able to see spirits in the aura, as well as "read" your state of health, emotions, and a great deal more about you from the aura's shape and color. Some books go beyond the usual explanations of what the colors mean and reveal many fascinating facets of the aura: for example, how anger sends out murky red "arrows" to penetrate someone else's aura. There are several books on this subject listed in the bibliography. The more you understand the aura, the better you can protect yourself by maintaining a healthy one.

You can strengthen your aura by using the White Light technique. Ideally, you should use it routinely twice a day, before you get out of bed in the morning and just before you go to sleep at night. The more you use it, the stronger your aura becomes; I believe that each time you use it, the aura is incrementally strengthened.

The White Light technique takes only a few seconds to perform. It can be done anywhere, without any preparation. The following verbatim transcript is exactly what I teach my patients during the first session.

White Light Technique

> Using your creative imagination, imagine that you have a miniature sun, just like the sun in our solar system, deep in your solar plexus. This sun is radiating through every atom and cell of your being. It fills you with light to the tips of your fingers, the top of your head, and the soles of your feet. It shines through you and beyond you an arm's length in every direction—above your head, below your feet, out to the sides, creating an aura—a brilliant, dazzling, radiant White Light that completely surrounds and protects you from any negativity or harm.

Once you have familiarized yourself with the White Light technique, you can use it with just a thought—an intention—and instantly you'll be protected. Think of turning on a light by flicking a switch; you can turn on the inner sun and let it shine through you like a light bulb, just as easily and quickly. It is extremely important to have a total conviction that you are safe within your White Light aura. Your thoughts, either negative or positive, are powerful.

The vibrations of your aura vary constantly. They reflect your general state of being—your physical, mental, emotional and spiritual health. You should use the White Light technique when necessary. If you are confronted with any situation or person involving negativity, surround yourself with the White Light. For example, if someone is furious at you, shouts at you or berates you, this is an excellent time to throw extra protection around yourself. Besides creating a barrier from angry and negative vibrations, you are preventing your aura from slowing down, which could leave you vulnerable to possession.

Being upset, depressed, fearful, jealous, or envious are all poisons that change the color of your aura to murky, unpleasant ones—and slow it down. The stronger the negative emotions, the weaker your protection!

It is imperative that you keep yourself in as positive a state of mind as possible, with your life balanced in regard to work, play and rest. Spirits can enter a weakened aura as easily as someone can walk through an open door.

An excellent way to protect yourself is to avoid using "recreational" drugs and alcohol. The amount that weakens the aura varies from person to person and also depends on the energy level. Some of my patients have lowered their resistance with only two glasses of wine. Even getting "stoned" or drunk once can result in a possession that can last a lifetime!

Do not assume you can protect yourself with White Light while using alcohol or drugs! It may strengthen your aura somewhat, but certainly not enough to prevent possession; your aura's vibrations will be lowered immediately.

As you've seen throughout this book, possessions can occur after surgery or during hospitalizations. In order to protect yourself at these times, you should take a double approach: first use the White Light technique often, from the time you enter the hospital and throughout your stay. Use it immediately before you are anesthetized, and as you recover consciousness. Stay as relaxed and positive as possible while in the hospital. Then, after you regain your strength, do a self-depossession, or have another person do one for you, just in case you picked up one or more spirits. This will help these confused entities to leave before they "settle in," and it will also prevent damaging effects to your aura's protective capacity—thereby avoiding further possession. This can be done in the hospital.

At funerals, and at all the events associated with them, you need extra protection around yourself. While at the funeral, or if viewing the body, mentally instruct the deceased to look for loved ones and to go to the Light. Tune into the room or location, and if you sense or detect other spirits, urge them to go to the spirit world.

Sometimes it is helpful to inform the one who has died of the circumstances of his death before continuing to educate him about going into the Light, etc. This helps to orient him to his new existence.

Prayers are very helpful. They call upon powerful sources of help—the highest. They may even enlist the aid of spiritual healers, doctors and specialists. Remember, "Ask and you shall receive." The Lord's Prayer is a potent means of protection. The Twenty-third Psalm is also excellent for this purpose. Say both of these prayers and you will be raising your aura's vibrations, as well as attracting help. If you are a non-Christian, say any prayer or affirmation with which you feel comfortable.

Since you are not dealing with demonic possession, using a cross, holy water or religious relics will not have any positive result, per se, with recalcitrant earthbound spirits. Imagine a stranger sitting in your living room. If he is stubborn and doesn't want to leave, putting a cross in front of him or sprinkling him with holy water wouldn't have the slightest effect. You would have to *persuade* him to leave. Since this book does not deal with the treatment of demonic spirits, I shall not comment on how useful crosses, holy water, etc., would be with these "heavy-weights." The bibliography does list books on this subject.

Summary of Major Means of Protection

1. Use the White Light technique twice daily.
2. Maintain a positive attitude.
3. Abstain from drugs and alcohol.
4. Use the White Light technique before surgery and during hospitalization.
5. Do a depossession immediately after surgery or hospitalization.
6. Pray and ask for spiritual help.

The next chapter deals with nonpossessing spirits—discarnates—who are either residents or visitors in your home. As they can be frightening or pose a threat of potential possession, you need to be aware of their presence, what to do about the condition, and how to protect your home.

16 * Detecting, Releasing, and Protecting Your Home from Spirits

Ghosts roaming castle corridors or making their presence known in homes have been the topic of stories that have fascinated people for centuries. Library shelves full of books about spirits attest to the lasting appeal of the hope that personality does survive death.

We all have had or at least have heard first-hand accounts of people who have seen spirits, had conversations with them, or had strange things happen in their homes—things that go "bump in the night"!

Why do spirits stay in a house or place? Why do they come uninvited? The answers are as various as are living people's reasons for being there.

Some stay because it was their home for many years and they feel comfortable in it. They wander around and tend to things, as they used to, usually unaware that they are dead.

A particularly sensitive patient told of buying an old Victorian house in San Francisco that had a reputation of being haunted. He could discern that there were six spirits, the former residents, and liked having them there. "They're not hurting anybody—and they're enjoying themselves."

Others stay because the new residence was built on the land where they once lived in a house or tent—or were buried. Many wander in, like hoboes finding free lodgings. Some, terrified, are glad to have a place to hide while they try to sort out what has happened to them. Spirit nomads wander from place to place and sometimes decide to stay because they like the living residents!

Without realizing it, people bring spirits along with them—and then they all make themselves at home!

Some places are populated with bands of discarnates. Others are drawn to these areas to join the ones already there. Two patients, living near canyons, told of many mishaps, fires, accidents, sightings of spirits and unfortunate deaths in these locations. A clairvoyant patient tuned into one canyon and saw hundreds of spirits, most of whom seemed to have been criminals, congregated in a gulch. We did an "absentee" depossession together and cleared it up—at least, so it seemed.

Graveyards are full of entities and should be entered only with the protection of the White Light technique.

Young children are much more able to see spirits than adults are, probably because they do not have beliefs that get in the way. Often these become their imaginary or invisible playmates, whom they have brought back from the hospital or picked up elsewhere. Sometimes they have died in the home and have remained there for years. Occasionally parents humor their children by actually setting places for them at the table, and holding mock conversations with these little "guests," as they would with anyone else in their households. Many patients under hypnosis trace back the origins of their possessions to interactions with these spirit friends.

Some survivors deliberately keep the deceased close to them with love and care. A patient confessed, "I never let Mother go—she's with me every day. I can feel her presence in the living room—and it's very comforting."

How to Detect Spirits in the Home

Over the years, I have found several prevalent and revealing signs that point to the presence of spirits in my patients' homes.

Strange Animal Behavior

Family pets can be extremely perceptive and responsive to earthbound entities. You may find them bristling and staring at something that you don't see. Your dog may growl, snarl, bark or run with its tail between its legs. Your cat may spit, every hair straight up with a full stiff tail. When spirits are in the house, the pet may refuse to enter a room, or slink around corners, "checking things out."

Moving Objects and other Unusual Happenings

Usually, it's not possible for spirits to move heavy objects, but at times they are able to manipulate small ones. One person mentioned finding the same teacup and spoon next to the sink every morning. Was a resident spirit having a cup of tea at night? Don't be frightened if you see something levitate or move. It may be an entity trying to catch your attention. Some are desperately seeking help. They need to have you know that they are there.

A friend told me of being badly frightened one Halloween night. She returned late to her apartment after attending a seance held once a year by stage magicians. As she was removing her makeup, her lipstick began moving erratically around the top of the dressing table. At first she thought there was an earthquake, but she realized immediately that nothing else was shaking. She then felt the presence of an uninvited guest. A phone call to her magician friend helped when he explained that the spirit was harmless and needed to be released. After she hung up, she prayed for help and was never disturbed again.

One of my most mediumistic patients, freighted down with troubled spirits, told me of a harrowing experience she had had since our last therapy session. As she was making a second trip into her kitchen from the car, unloading groceries, her feet slipped on shattered glass. Looking down, she saw fragments of a large lighting fixture that had been knocked off the ceiling and had crashed onto the counter near her first bag of groceries. It had smashed into hundreds of slivers. Because of the timing of the event, it seemed obvious to her that the entity wanted to attract her attention, but not to harm her.

We discovered that this spirit, a prostitute, was furious since she had been stabbed to death in a motel room when she demanded to be paid before having sex with her customer. Further conversations with her, and a little detective work by my patient, disclosed that her account corroborated a recent front-page news story. This entity had been one of many prostitutes murdered by a former policeman, who hid their bodies in oil drums. She wanted revenge! Ultimately, we talked her into leaving with loved ones.

This same patient, on other occasions, reported small plants being knocked off a living room table and the lights and TV turning on and off.

An interesting case involved a mischievous, male, teenage spirit who had lived with the children of one family, accompanied them into the home of their young friends, and then decided to stay there. He went to work the next day with the father and caused havoc by turning switches and endangering lives! This continued for several days until the employee was asked by his boss to keep his "tagalong" at home—or else! Fortunately, the entity got the message!

It is quite common for entities to affect lights, TVs and radios to call attention to themselves or to scare others deliberately.

Knocks and Raps

Spirits knock on walls and other objects to let you know they are there. Sometimes they spell out messages, often their names, using a code: one rap represents "A," two "B," three "C" and so on; or one rap for "yes," two for "no" and three for "maybe" or "uncertain." Usually these are bids for help, but occasionally they are playful or even malicious attempts to frighten the occupants of the mutually shared home.

Miscellaneous Unusual Happenings

Many strange things happen as a result of spirit visitors. Books, keys and other items disappear, only to reappear later. The following account is one of the strangest I've ever heard:

One of my patients reported an event that, had she not known about spirits, would have caused her to question her sanity.

As she was watching the eleven o'clock news, she heard a

loud explosion in her house, and felt some mild vibrations. She quickly went from room to room, looking for the source of the noise. Since everything was as it should be, she became extremely apprehensive. Then she heard water "trickling." She assumed a water pipe had burst, but then remembered that the explosion didn't sound like it came from behind the wall. She checked the kitchen sink and her bathroom—and could find nothing out of order. She thought to look into the rarely used guest bathroom.

To her horror, she saw the glass shower door shattering! It continued to shatter—for forty minutes! The sound she thought was water trickling was the shower door crackling. Realizing nothing "normal" could cause that, she immediately thought of spirits. She then became calm—all the anxiety left instantly. She surrounded herself with White Light and went into her bedroom. Playing the depossession tape I had made for her, she went off to sleep peacefully.

I saw her the next day for her regularly scheduled appointment. After making a tape (see the transcript in the next section) for her to play in the bathroom—and elsewhere, if necessary, I placed her under hypnosis, and asked her about the spirit.

She described him as a sandy-haired, pleasant man of thirty-four. He had shattered her shower door because it was the only thing he could do that she could not have explained away. She reasoned that he wanted to attract attention to enlist her help. Furthermore, she assumed that he had come with her ex-husband, who had spent the afternoon visiting her. Since he wasn't feeling well, she played her relaxation tape for him. It was at that time that the entity left him and became an uninvited guest in her home.

Cold Spots

Cold spots in your home may be indications of spirits. Some remain in the same location, others seem to move around.

Seeing Spirits

Patients reported seeing shadows moving or people who seemed very real. Sometimes this happened only when they were alone, but on other occasions spirits were seen by several people.

Others told of being awakened from a sound sleep to see a person at the foot of their beds. Even when they recognized deceased loved ones, many were terrified and rudely ordered them to leave immediately. If the intruder looked menacing, it was especially frightening.

A patient mentioned waking up with a start to see a man with a black, charred face staring at her. She panicked and screamed—and he departed. Later, she and her sister figured out that the spirit was someone they had come to know about when they visited their dying father in the hospital. They had comforted the family of a young man who was in a coma, badly burned and fatally injured from a motorcycle accident. After his death he apparently accompanied my patient to her home. Once she realized who he was, she understood how unwarranted her panic had been. She talked to him and he left.

Being Touched by Spirits

Spirits can touch people. Have you ever felt something like cobwebs across your face? Or a cold caress? Sometimes these are strong enough to be considered a push or a light hit. Don't be alarmed. Remember, they cannot harm you. It could be a loved one trying to let you know he or she is there. Notice how often living people touch each other, even giving friendly punches at times.

Hearing Spirits

Years ago I awakened from a deep sleep to hear my name being called. It sounded like a voice in the room, definitely not a thought within my own head. Since then, my patients and friends have told me of hearing voices—usually addressing them by name, delivering messages or asking for help.

If you suspect there is a spirit in your home, you can do a bit of detective work and set up your tape recorder with a blank tape and a timer for late at night, and you might find a message the next morning. If it is voice-activated, better still. Spirits have been recorded, and there are references on this in the bibliography.

Smelling Spirits

Sometimes spirits can be detected by odors. The most common are perfume, after-shave lotion, cigarettes, cigars and pipe tobacco. These smells often help people to recognize their "guests." For example, if your mother is on the "other side" and you notice her favorite fragrance, it may be that she is either visiting you or trapped in the physical world without a body. Entities who are not earthbound but just dropping in to pay a visit may deliberately bring their identifying scents so that you will know them.

However, discarnates who have not left the earth plane occasionally have odors accompanying them. Patients have reported medicinal smells, for example, ones that reminded them of their parents' hospital rooms. Other reported smelling their fathers' favorite pipe tobaccos or mothers' colognes.

How to Release Spirits from Your Home

If you know who the spirits are, talk to them lovingly and explain that their bodies are dead, and explain how they died; tell them that their loved ones are here with them to take them to the spirit world. Then bless them and tell them to leave. Use the same format that you learned in chapter 13.

One kindly patient explained to a recent spirit visitor that it was not his home, but hers. She explained that nothing in the room looked familiar to him, pointing out various objects to impress upon him the reality of the situation. He left very quickly.

Record the following transcript or put the same ideas in your own words. The one I have designed is for general use. If you know—or suspect—who the entity is, tailor your own recording to fit the circumstances. For example, if you know how the person died, include that in your "talk" to him or her. If you have an idea of who would come from the spirit world to help—a parent, spouse, or sibling, etc., call attention to that loved one.

Generalized Transcript for Clearing a Residence

You are here in this home as an earthbound spirit. Do you remember when you were in your own body? (Pause.) Well, it died. But *you* didn't die—just your body did. You will never die.

When your body died, you should have gone immediately into the spirit world. In fact, your loved ones came at that time to help you. If you had gone then, all of this time you would have been living a wonderful, happy life. You would have been with your loved ones—family and friends. You would never have been alone.

Instead, you remained here in the physical world *without any body!* That's why people don't see you or hear you. You are an invisible spirit. It must have been very confusing and lonely for you all this time.

Now you're going to be helped. Notice who's here! Your loved ones. (Pause.) They are overjoyed to see you, because they have been very worried about you. You thought you would never see them again when they went through the death process. But here they are, very much *alive*. They came to help you. They are smiling at you. Now they are putting their arms around you—holding you. (Pause.) You can feel their love. (Pause.) They are holding your hand—and will stay with you. You no longer will be alone.

Notice how warm and real their hands are. They are in their spirit bodies. And you too will be in your own spirit body in just a few minutes. It will be a perfect body in every way. It will not age or get sick. There will be no aches and pains. It will be a youthful, attractive body.

Your loved ones are going to take you to that beautiful Light over there. (Pause.) The moment you enter the Light, you will be in your perfect, youthful body. Then you all will go together into the spirit world.

You can have everything you want in your new life—love, happiness, food, drink, sex. You can have fun, if you like. *It's a very real world!* Your loved ones are going to tell you about it now. (Long pause.)

Many people are afraid of going to hell. But there is *no such place as hell!* You do not have to take my word for it. There is a teacher of religious education from the spirit world here to help you understand that there is no hell—that you have nothing to fear. (Long pause.)

The worst is behind you. And a wonderful, peaceful, beautiful life is ahead of you.

There are more loved ones and helpers here now. They are going to show you how to go to the Light. They will go with you. They will stay with you. You will not be alone.

I (We) forgive you for any harm you have done here in this home. I (We) send you to your new life with blessings and love.

Go now! In the name of the Father, the Son, Jesus Christ, and the Holy Spirit, go in peace, and Light, and love. *Leave now!*

I prefer to do the blessing at the end, but if you feel uncomfortable with it, it is not essential. I believe it raises the vibrations and adds positivity. You may use any blessing that seems appropriate.

The recording may be played at any time, or as many times as you feel are necessary. Like a depossession, sometimes it takes a while for a spirit to understand the message or to overcome fear or indecision.

You may prefer to attach your tape recorder to a timer, and play it while you are out of your residence. If the spirits are more active at a certain time of the day or night, play it at that time. Also, if you believe there is an entity in a particular place or room, play it there.

If you find that your uninvited guests have no intention of leaving, you may have to find a local medium or clairvoyant to come to your home and make contact with them. He or she will usually be able to convince the spirits to leave. If this doesn't work at first, try again with other psychics.

Dowsers also may prove very helpful, not only to ascertain if there are spirits and if so, how many, but what intentions they have and why they are there. Some talented dowsers, besides being able to clear the home and property, even claim to be able to create a protective wall around the formerly afflicted property.

Dowsers can be found by contacting the American Society of Dowsers, Danville, VT 05828-0024.

Some patients report excellent results by ordering spirits to leave, especially if they find them at the foot of their beds after waking up at night. They command them to leave in the name of Jesus Christ. They also calm themselves by reciting the Lord's Prayer or the Twenty-third Psalm.

As mentioned earlier, this usually does not work in depossessing oneself or another, but it occasionally does achieve the desired results in this sort of situation. Perhaps the spirits leave because they are shocked by the response of the person, or because they realize they have badly frightened someone. It may solve the immediate problem, but it will not help the entity to go into the spirit world, which should be your ultimate goal.

How to Protect Your Home from Spirits

1. *Do not invite spirits into your home!* Therefore, do not arrange seances, use the Ouija board, or do automatic writing. The potential disasters that may result definitely outweigh any possible benefits.

2. Do not use drugs (marijuana, heroin, cocaine, etc.) or abuse alcohol in your home. Undesirable spirits may be attracted to your residence and possibly to your aura and your body.

3. Surround your home daily with White Light. Imagine a halo or aura of bright White Light surrounding it completely. *Know* that it is totally protected from spirits—or any negativity or harm.

4. Imagine each room filled with White Light. It only takes a minute. Do it daily.

5. Ask mentally or verbally for protection from higher beings: i.e., Jesus Christ, the Lord or spirit guides.

6. Keep your home happy and filled with love. Some spirits feed on the energy from fights and hostility. Bursts of energy

from these explosions provide a banquet for energy-weakened entities.

The spirits I have been describing are just residents, not possessors. However, they can slip into and out of the auras and bodies of living people if the opportunities arise, as described in chapter 11.

Also, some entities have the ability to come and go and to possess different people, one at a time, as they wish. I have treated an addicted spirit, seeking highs from novocaine, who went to the dentist within the bodies of two members of the same family—and even the neighbor across the street!

Remember that having spirits in your home is not a catastrophe. Much worse things could happen to you. It is a situation that exists, a problem to be solved. And it can be solved, as you have seen.

17 * Some Further Thoughts on the Unquiet Dead

Is spirit possession a fantasy? Or is it the prevalent and potentially disastrous condition that has been described in *The Unquiet Dead?* After all the years I've worked with spirits, often "wrestling" with ones who are stubborn, confused, hostile and terrified, I'm still not one hundred percent convinced that they are not figments of the imagination. As a therapist, the question is moot—the therapy works. As a person, the issue is an exceedingly important one, because it has far-reaching implications.

The conviction that spirits possess living people is based on the premise that *life does continue after death*. Earthbound entities are simply those who did not make the natural transition to the higher planes of existence. Possession shows us that only the physical body dies and that personality survives—that we are immortal beings.

One of the most frequent and serious criticisms of the viewpoint that spirits are the source of a great deal of human misery is that it is an abdication of personal responsibility. We blame spirits, when we ourselves are the cause of our bad deeds, problems and symptoms. Besides absolving ourselves, this attitude (believing spirits to be responsible) precludes taking action to make necessary changes.

If, on the other hand, the concept is based in reality, then the issue of responsibility becomes muddied. To what degree are we held accountable for what we do, if we are controlled by spirits and are in fact "helpless" pawns? Our courts recognize freedom from responsibility for our actions if we are adjudged insane. If our personalities are overwhelmed by those of our possessors, are we innocent by virtue of possession? Since it is a matter of degree, do we accept the responsibility for only some of our actions and problems?

Before my work with depossession, I was always puzzled when I heard of a man killing his whole family and then himself. Often there was no obvious motivation for the tragedy. Many times the murderer was an upstanding citizen, even a pillar of his church, loved and respected by those who knew him well. How many murders, suicides, incidents of child abuse and other crimes are committed by possessing spirits?

Assuming that possession is real, how prevalent is it? Is everyone possessed—at least at some point? What percent of the population has this affliction? In anyone's life there are multitudinous situations or conditions that weaken the aura; for example my findings indicate that being drunk or under the influence of drugs only *one time* has led to possession.

How populated with discarnates is our physical world? Why have so many spirits remained here? Are these entities the dregs of humanity, like sediment, staying at a denser level of vibrations? Interestingly, I never have conversed with a spiritually evolved possessing entity. Those must go automatically into the spirit world following their deaths.

How do earthbound spirits move from one location to another? These lost souls appear to be as limited in their ability to travel as we are. They seem to go from one place to another by the same means. From my work I have found them traveling in cars, some have even gone by jets!

Possession can help us to understand abnormal behavior, personality, mental, emotional and physical problems. How many patients who are in mental institutions are *not* psychotic, but possessed? Are the voices they hear real? How much physical suffering is the continuance of the spirits' own pains and symptoms at their deaths?

Are unexplained spontaneous remissions from physical and emotional symptoms the result of the departure of a possessing spirit? I talked to a musician who told me about his depression. Seeing no results, after several years he finally discontinued his therapy. Then, years later, he awoke one morning relieved of his depression and hasn't been troubled with it since.

I wonder if some of the miraculous healings that do occur with powerful healers are not a driving out of possessing spirits—very like Carl Wickland's technique with electroshock, described in his *Thirty Years Among the Dead*. I regressed a patient who did benefit from a healing of this sort—the healer had put her hand on his head and shouted, "You are healed!" He was caught by her assistants as he swooned and woke up a few minutes later on the floor of the auditorium. He recalled under hypnosis several entities being released from him and having been taken away by helping spirits who were working with the healer.

I feel that the concept of possession needs to be included in the course material (in abnormal psychology, psychiatry, etc.) at our colleges, universities and medical schools. Research should be undertaken to broaden our understanding of the role that spirits play in human life. Information on possession should be made public in order that people may protect themselves better, as well as understand what is happening to them and get help.

Depossession is growing as a therapeutic tool. I have trained over one hundred mental health professionals and physicians in the United States and more than sixty in Brazil. The people I have trained are training others. Besides these, many professionals and nonprofessionals, like metaphysical and Spiritualist ministers, as well as psychics, mediums and shamans, have been using variations of these techniques for decades, hundreds, even thousands of years.

Depossession therapy, by whatever name, is spreading because it is extremely effective and efficient. Fortunately, neither the therapist nor patient needs to believe in spirits or possession for it to work. Some healers are able to use it telepathically without the possessed even being in their presence—usually they do not know it is being done.

Although it can produce "miracles," it is *not* a panacea. Even when the cause of the condition is clearly possession, depossession therapy sometimes doesn't result in a cure. There are powerful forces within the mind—those of the patients and those of the spirits who are possessing them. In some unfortunate cases, deep-seated needs perpetuate the possession. Of course, these are treated, but may not result in a relinquishing of the condition.

Often, before it even gets to that stage of therapy, the patient terminates the treatment—to escape the cure!

One of the issues involved in depossession therapy is the role of suggestion—hypnotic or nonhypnotic. I have struggled with my fear of implanting suggestions of possession when I was not even sure there was such a condition. Also, with some patients, the diagnosis is not clear-cut. I tell my patients that I'm not convinced of the validity of possession, but I ask them to use it as a working hypothesis as I have. Even so, hypnosis is powerful and I do not want to create a problem when one does not exist. As with many psychotherapeutic decisions, there is a blend of expertise, intuition and common sense.

If spirits incorrectly are blamed for problems, the person may not seek appropriate help. This would be especially serious in cases where physical symptoms are seen as the result of spirit intervention.

I find dramatically positive changes in people using these techniques, and I have *not* found any lasting negative results. Depossession can stir things up, because the underlying causes, possessing entities, are unmasked and they may feel threatened and upset. But the spirits have been there all along, and their reactions are temporary.

When the therapy is lengthy and the spirits do not leave after a few sessions, I generally find that the possessor and the possessed have been together in past lifetimes! The motivations for the possession may be found in events from the previous times they have been together. There may be a burning desire for revenge on one or both parts. The possessee may keep the spirit trapped as punishment. On the other hand, there may be a powerful attachment between the two based on mutual love and/or dependency. For example, the spirit may have been the mother of the person in another incarnation and possessed him or her in childhood. In most instances, neither is aware of the subconscious memories of the previous lives they have shared—or the real reasons for the possessions.

I find that in every case that is investigated, the possessee has possessed another in an earlier lifetime—deliberately or unwittingly.

This brings up the issue of karma. Is every possessed person paying off a karmic debt? Are the two, the possessor and the possessee, invariably in a karmic relationship? If not, are past lives always involved in possession?

Some people appear to stay possessed—once the diagnosis has been clearly made—despite all attempts at depossessions, despite the exploration of past-life connections and motivations for being possessed, and despite the help of absentee healers who specialize in long-distance depossessions. I always assume more work needs to be done to free these people. It's hard for me to give up helping them.

The issue of free will must be considered in possession. On the surface, it looks like we're puppets, manipulated against our wills by spirits or fate. Did we agree to have this experience when we planned our lives in the interims between our last deaths and before our births? Are we really only "meeting ourselves"? Have we in every case possessed someone else before?

Many of the questions that I've raised in this chapter cannot be answered because of our limited understanding and knowledge of spirits, possession, reincarnation and universal laws.

I have shared with you my points of view, and have given you techniques that work. I feel that an understanding of the spiritual dimension of life can enhance our freedom to live life to its fullest. My deepest wish for you and/or your loved ones is freedom from possession. Even if you just have new hope or have considered a different way of looking at human suffering, my book has served its purpose.

18 * Questions and Answers

These questions are those most frequently asked during my lectures on spirit possession.

1. Why are the loved ones from the spirit world not there when people die, to prevent them from becoming earthbound?

The spirit loved ones *are* present at that time, trying to attract the attention of the earthbound spirits, which they continue to do, off and on, for many years. The problem is that the newly deceased are too confused to see them, or they resist the help because of their desires to remain in the physical world. Sometimes they do see them but are too ashamed to relate to them. This is especially the case if there's been a suicide.

2. How long do spirits remain earthbound without possessing someone or before going into the spirit world?

There is a lot of variation in the lengths of their stays in the physical world as discarnates. It appears that most are rescued by higher, helping spirits, when they are ready to relinquish their ties to the material world or when they become aware of their condition, i.e., that their bodies have died. Most remain for ten years or less before possessing someone or going into the next life. I have found one who remained earthbound for forty years before possessing my patient. He spent that time just "wandering." Of course, we have all heard about ghosts who haunt buildings for hundreds of years. I do believe some of these stories are true.

3. How do you explain "multiple personalities," as described in The Three Faces of Eve*?*

My view is that these cases are probably uncontrolled mediums who are multiply possessed. The "personalities" are actually other people—spirits. The reason these patients are generally unresponsive to therapy—at least with lasting cures—is that the main cause, possession, is not treated. When it is, the "personalities" disappear.

4. Can a person consciously call spirits in, resulting in possession or their continuing presence in the home?

Definitely! This is often the problem after the death of family members or other loved ones. Sometimes, lonely people deliberately ask spirits to join them. Others seek advice or help, not realizing that when the call goes out, anyone can answer. Ouija boards, automatic writing and seances are also ways that spirits incorporate with permission.

5. What happens to people who commit suicide?

From the work I've done, I find that some remain in the physical world as discarnates, carrying all the heavy feelings they experienced moments before their deaths. As long as they are earthbound, they feel exactly as they did prior to the suicide.

Others who kill themselves go directly into the Light and the spirit world. The moment they float up from their lifeless bodies, they feel free and relieved of their depression, anguish or anger.

Those who go into the Light immediately and those who remain in the physical world ultimately have to face the same test situation: the choice of killing themselves or not. Like an exam, they either fail it again, in another life, or pass it by not destroying themselves. There is no punishment, only education and other chances for spiritual growth.

6. Have any of the people you have regressed to former lives found themselves in hell after their deaths?

I have performed between twenty and thirty thousand individual past-life regressions, and never found one single case when a spirit was in a situation approximating the popular concept of hell. Some remain in a "hell" because they continued to suffer what they had experienced before their deaths. Others were trapped in the bodies of those they possessed and—in my opinion—that must be a "hell." They could not live their own lives, or be their own persons—exactly what they inflicted on their possessees.

7. Are schizophrenics really possessed, rather than psychotic?

I feel that the majority of patients in mental institutions are presenting their symptoms because they are possessed. The voices they hear are real; some of the visual hallucinations are glimpses of the lower astral plane, a part of the spirit world that is of a very dense vibratory nature. There is still a great deal to learn about these extreme cases of mental derangement. I do *not* feel that all schizophrenics are psychotic, *because* of the possibility of possession. I do feel that—in addition to their mental illness—they are undoubtedly possessed. The possession is an extra burden for them.

8. If one has trouble "seeing" the White Light when using the White Light technique for protection, is this preventing it from being effective?

No, many of my patients don't "see" the White Light when they are strengthening their auras. Just imagining it is there, or *knowing* it is there is enough.

9. How can I tell the difference between a nonearthbound spirit and one who is likely to possess me? I'm especially interested in the difference in regard to a loved one who has died.

A spirit who has gone into the Light and the afterlife and returned for a "visit" would *never* enter your body or aura, unless you were a trained and developed medium being used by highly evolved spirits.

It is difficult to tell the difference between, say, your mother coming from the spirit world to give you a message and her being in your home because she is earthbound.

One way to make that discrimination would be to notice the feeling or tone of her presence. If it is positive, loving, and nonclinging, then, probably, she is not earthbound. If it seems heavy, sad, anxious or angry, then you can be sure that she is.

To be on the safe side, advise her that she has died, and tell her to go to her new life with the loved ones who are there to help her. If she has come from the spirit world to be of service or to say "hello," she will not be affronted and will fulfill her purpose.

10. How can you tell the difference between a spirit guide and an earthbound spirit?

In the presence of a spirit guide, you would always feel a lot of positive energy—you would feel good. With an earthbound discarnate, you would feel drained, anxious or scared.

Again, sometimes it is difficult to tell the difference by judging your reactions, because many people are afraid of spirits who are not earthbound, even if they are guides or loved ones. They get "spooked," just because they are encountering something unfamiliar.

11. What is the difference between a "walk-in" and a possessing entity?

Ruth Montgomery has described the "walk-in" phenomenon in several of her latest books. Briefly, there is an agreement made at a soul level (between the higher self and the evolved spirit who wishes to incarnate) between living people who no longer wish to remain in their own bodies (or who are going to die shortly) and highly developed souls who want to contribute to our world and who prefer not to go through a lengthy childhood and early adulthood. The former leave, and the latter, the walk-ins, take over.

In the case of possession, the original inhabitants, the possessed, do not leave their bodies, and the cohabitation *never* is a positive solution. The possessees and the possessors are mutually hurt by this condition—despite what either may claim!

12. Who are invisible or imaginary playmates?

They are actually discarnates—spirits who have not made their transitions to the afterlife. Because children are unusually clairvoyant and clairaudient—very much like animals—they "see" and "hear" these entities. They believe they are living children, as do the spirits themselves who do not understand their situation. They become friends, especially since the entities are very lonely and confused—being stranded on the earth plane. Often, these spirits later possess their friends, sometimes unknowingly. In these cases, often the possessees do not want to release their possessors. Of course, this is subconsciously motivated. Once the identity and history of the spirit are available to the conscious mind by the possessed, a depossession usually is easily carried out.

13. How does possession relate to the concept of free will?

My understanding is still somewhat incomplete regarding this issue.

It could be that *all* possession is *subconsciously* allowed. If that were the case, free will would still be operating. In the cases that I have explored, it does appear that in the majority, the possession *was* allowed—mainly at a subconscious level, occasionally at a conscious one.

Another speculation is that the possession is arranged during the interim—between death and rebirth—for karmic reasons or for the lessons involved.

The third possibility is that the concept of free will is invalid—that we are pawns, manipulated by circumstances.

Lastly, perhaps the possession itself is a fantasy.

14. What happens to possessing entities when the possessees die?

In most cases they remain earthbound, as discarnates. Then after some time, they "join" someone else. I've treated a number who—in total—possessed four or five people consecutively.

In a few regressions, I've seen that their "hosts"—upon releasing from their bodies—have taken them into the Light with them. This happens especially if the spirits are known to them—parents, spouses, friends, etc. Sometimes, the spirit loved ones of the possessees take the possessing entities along with them. Then they all go into the spirit world together.

15. Do children who have died grow up in the spirit world?

Yes, from regressions, it appears that they do grow up when they make their proper transitions. Unfortunately, some remain earthbound as discarnates or possessors, in which case they do not grow up. This accounts for some of the childish behavior, interests, limitations and reactions of people who are possessed by children. They are often afraid to drive or do grown-up activities.

* Glossary

Astral body: A body vibrating at a higher frequency than the physical body. It is believed that a living human being has an astral body as well as a physical one. It is sometimes referred to as the "emotional body."

Astral plane* or *world: The next dimension above the physical plane or world. It is populated by spirits and seems to them to be a replica of the physical world. There are various levels of the astral plane: The major divisions are the lower astral and the higher astral.

Aura: An invisible electromagnetic force field that emanates from living people, animals and plants. It reflects health, thoughts, emotions and other information. One of its main functions is to protect the individual from outside negative influences, including discarnates.

Automatic writing: Writing performed by spirits using and controlling the hand of a living person. This can be done with a pencil, pen, typewriter or word processor.

Channeling: Allowing a spirit from the higher planes to manifest through a medium's physical body; most commonly, by speaking, writing, painting, playing a musical instrument or healing others, even performing "surgery."

Clairaudience: The ability to psychically hear what lies beyond physical sound.

Clairvoyance: The ability to psychically see what lies beyond normal sight.

Clinical-death experience: Actually dying, even in some cases being medically pronounced dead, and either reviving spontaneously or being brought back to life through resuscitation or other medical means. Often people remember these experiences, which usually are the highlights of their lives.

Demon: A creature of evil nature from another dimension.

Discarnate: A spirit who is trapped in the physical world, i.e., not the higher planes, without his or her physical body. Used synonymously in this book with "spirit" and "entity."

Dowser: A person who has a psychic talent to discern unseen things (underground water, oil, mineral deposits, health, entities, etc.) through the use of a pendulum, a forked branch or a metal rod. Such a person is commonly called a "water witch."

Earthbound: A condition of remaining in the physical world as a spirit after the death of the body because of not having made a successful transition into the higher realms. According to esoteric theory, an earthbound entity is actually trapped in the lower astral plane.

Entity: The immortal essence of a person. It is used synonymously in this book with "spirit" and "discarnate."

Esoteric: That which pertains to metaphysical concepts.

Exorcism: A rite to force possessing spirits, especially of a satanic or demonic nature, from a living person or object, including a house.

Exorcist: A highly trained specialist, usually a Catholic priest, who uses a prescribed ritual to force a possessing satanic or demonic influence to leave the possessed.

Extrasensory perception (ESP): The knowledge of facts, happenings, or presences through means other than the five senses of the physical body.

Finger signals: A communication system that is established by a hypnotist with the subconscious mind of the subject. The inner mind is temporarily in control of the hands and selects fingers to represent "yes," "no," and "I don't want to answer."

Hypnosis: A state of mind that is highly responsive to suggestion, used to redirect and influence mental activity, and hence behavior and emotions.

Hypnotic regression: A hypnotic technique that produces the remembering and reliving of a past experience from the current life or a previous one, the memory of which is buried in the subconscious.

Hypnotic suggestion: Ideas presented to the subconscious mind while in the hypnotic state.

Incorporation: The entering into a physical body of a living human being by a discarnate; the act of possession.

Induction: A process for creating the state of hypnosis; usually it is a verbal technique producing deep relaxation and responsiveness to suggestions.

Karma: An ancient concept embodying the principle that you reap what you sow—the law of cause and effect—it implies that you are always meeting yourself. Karma can be positive as well as negative.

Levitate: To lift physical objects by psychic force.

Lower astral body: The vehicle in which you exist following the death of the physical body if the spirit remains in the material world, i.e., it does not make a successful transition to the spirit world. It corresponds to the lower planes of consciousness: the lower astral plane.

Medium: A person who is sensitive psychically and able to communicate with spirits and produce manifestations.

Metaphysics: That which lies beyond the realm of physics (physical experience); sometimes considered the occult. Some areas of general interest in metaphysics are reincarnation, possession, levels of existence, auras, spirit guides, mediumship, crystal and pyramid power, astrology, etc.

Near-death experience: The experience of actually having nearly died; having suffered "clinical" death; the loss of all vital signs, like heartbeat and respiration. Synonymous with the clinical death experience.

Ouija board: A board printed with the alphabet, "yes," "no," and numbers, and a planchette (see below), which moves on the board spelling out messages; used for contacting spirits.

Out-of-body-experience (OBE): The spirit body travels while still connected to the physical body by the "silver cord." Sometimes referred to as astral projection or soul travel.

Past-life therapy: Psychotherapy that involves regressions to former lifetimes in order to solve current problems.

Pendulum: An object that is used to discern the answer to posed questions. It usually consists of a small round or pointed object suspended on a short chain or string. It moves by subconscious direction.

Planchette: A device used with the Ouija board. It is a small triangular or heart-shaped board with short legs and a pointer.

Psychic: A person who is sensitive to perceptions other than those received through the five physical senses.

Psychic surgery: Surgical operations performed on the human body through a medium.

Raps: Sounds made by spirits that are produced by psychic energy on a physical object.

Reincarnation: The return to physical existence by the soul in repeated existences.

Repression: A defense mechanism of the mind in which there is a "forgetting" of an experience that is painful emotionally or physically. It is automatic and is not related to age; you can repress a memory at any age. It is not ordinary forgetting, but serves a protective purpose. It can be overcome by various means. In this book, hypnosis is used to uncover repressed memories.

Roman Ritual: The official ritual used by Catholic priests during an exorcism.

Seance: A special meeting for spirit communication or demonstration of psychic phenomena over which a medium usually presides.

Sensitive: A person who has psychic abilities.

Shaman: Commonly known as a "medicine man—or a "witch doctor"—one who uses ancient techniques to achieve and maintain well-being and healing for himself and for members of his community.

Silver cord: An energy form that connects the spirit to the physical body. It is clairvoyantly perceived as a silver-colored cord that is attached to the spirit when it travels out of the physical body.

Somnambulism: A very deep state of hypnosis characterized by amnesia (loss of memory). Another form is nocturnal sleepwalking.

Spirit: The immortal essence of a person. The term generally is used in this book interchangeably with "discarnate" and "entity."

Spirit guides: Highly evolved souls from the spirit world who have elected to help living people. They can also be deceased loved ones who have made successful transitions to the afterlife, who return to give aid and guidance from time to time. They do not intrude into the auras or bodies of individuals whom they are helping.

Spirit world: The realm of life which is populated by spirits who have gone into the Light and made a successful transition from the physical world. It is a plane of existence generally regarded as vibrating at a higher frequency than the physical world.

Subconscious: The part of the mind that functions below the threshold of consciousness. The "subconscious" mind referred to in this book is able to store memories of everything that has been experienced exactly as it was perceived at the time.

Tarot cards: A deck of cards designed to reveal the past, present and future of the participant. The various configurations are interpreted by a psychic reader.

Telepathy: The psychic transmission and reception of thoughts.

Trance: A sleeplike state in which there is a lessening of consciousness. It can vary from slight to extremely deep. It can be hypnotic or nonhypnotic.

Trance mediums: Sensitives who lose consciousness and are temporarily and willingly possessed by spirits wishing to communicate or to heal.

* Bibliography

Allison, R. 1980. *Mind in Many Pieces*. New York: Rawson, Wade.
Bagnall, O. 1975. *The Origins and Properties of the Human Aura*. New York: Weiser.
Banerjee, H. N. 1980. *Americans Who Have Been Reincarnated*. New York: Macmillan.
Brandon, R. 1983. *The Spiritualists*. New York: Random House.
Brittle, G. 1981. *The Demonologist*. New York: Berkley.
———. 1983. *The Devil in Connecticut*. New York: Bantam.
Brown, R. 1975. *Immortals by My Side*. Chicago: Henry Regnery.
———. 1971. *Unfinished Symphonies*. New York: Morrow.
Budge, W. E. A. 1967. *The Egyption Book of the Dead*. New York: Dover.
Cannon, A. 1954. *The Invisible Influence*. New York: Dutton.
Cerminara, G. 1950. *Many Mansions*. New York: Morrow.
———. 1963. *Many Lives, Many Loves*. New York: Morrow.
Chaplin, A. 1977. *The Bright Light of Death*. Marina del Rey: DeVorss.
Crabtree, A. 1985. *Multiple Man: Explorations in Possession and Multiple Personality*. New York: Praeger.
Davis, W. 1980. *Dojo-Magic and Exorcism in Modern Japan*. Stanford: Stanford University Press.
Dethlefsen, T. 1976. *Voices from Other Lives*. New York: Evans.
Doyle, A. C. 1926. *History of Spiritualism*. New York: Cassell.

Ebon, M., editor. 1974. *Exorcism: Fact Not Fiction*. New York: New American Library.
———. 1977. *The Evidence for Life After Death*. New York: New American Library.
Evans-Wentz, W. Y. 1960. *The Tibetan Book of the Dead*. Oxford: Oxford University Press.
Fiore, E. 1977. *You Have Been Here Before*. New York: Coward-McCann.
Fodor, N. 1959. *The Haunted Mind*. New York: Garrett.
Fortune, D. 1930. *Psychic Self-defense*. London: Aquarian Press.
Guirdham, A. 1982. *The Psychic Dimensions of Mental Health*. Wellingborough: Thurstone Press.
Harner, M. 1980. *The Way of the Shaman*. New York: Harper & Row.
Head, J. and S. R. Cranston. 1968. *Reincarnation: An East-West Anthology*. Wheaton, Ill.: Quest.
Holzer, H. 1974. *The Reincarnation Primer: Patterns of Destiny*. New York: Harper & Row.
Kardec, A. 1898. *The Spirits' Book*. London: Psychic Press.
Kelsey, D. and J. Grant. 1967. *Many Lifetimes*. Garden City, N.Y.: Doubleday.
Kübler-Ross, E. 1969. *On Death and Dying*. New York: Macmillan.
———. 1981. *Living with Death and Dying*. New York: Macmillan.
Kuhn, A. 1939. *Theosophy: A Modern Revival of Ancient Wisdom*. New York: Holt.
Kuthumi. 1971. *Studies of the Human Aura*. Colorado Springs: Summit Lighthouse.
Leadbeater, C. W. 1903. *Clairvoyance*. Madras, India: The Theosophical Publishing House.
Leeks, S. 1975. *Driving Out the Devils*. New York: Putnam.
LeShan, L. 1974. *The Medium, the Mystic and the Physicist*. New York: Viking.
MacLaine, S. 1983. *Out on a Limb*. New York: Bantam.
———. 1985. *Dancing in the Light*. New York: Bantam.
Manning, M. 1975. *The Link: Matthew Manning's Own Story of His Extraordinary Gifts*. New York: Holt, Rinehart & Winston.

Martin, M. 1976. *Hostage to the Devil*. New York: Reader's Digest.

Mishlove, J. 1975. *The Roots of Consciousness*. New York: Random House.

Montgomery, J. W., editor. 1976. *Demon Possession: A Medical, Historical, Anthropological and Theological Symposium*. Minneapolis: Bethany House.

Montgomery, R. 1966. *A Search for the Truth*. New York: Ballantine.

———. 1968. *Here and Hereafter*. New York: Ballantine.

———. 1971. *A World Beyond*. Greenwich, Conn.: Fawcett.

———. 1974. *Companions Along the Way*. New York: Ballantine.

———. 1976. *A World Before*. New York: Ballantine.

———. 1979. *Strangers Among Us*. New York: Ballantine.

———. 1982. *Threshold to Tomorrow*. New York: Ballantine.

——— and J. Garland. 1986. *Ruth Montgomery: Herald of the New Age*. Garden City, N.Y.: Doubleday/Dolphin.

Moody, R. 1975. *Life After Life*. Atlanta: Mockingbird Press.

Muldoon, S. and H. Carrington. 1970. *The Projection of the Astral Body*. New York: Weiser.

Myer, F. W. H. 1954. *The Human Personality and Its Survival of Bodily Death*. New York: Longmans, Green.

Netherton, M. and N. Shiffrin. 1978. *Past Lives Therapy*. New York: Morrow.

Osis, K. and E. Haraldsson. 1977. *At the Hour of Death*. New York: Avon.

Powell, A. E. 1925. *The Etheric Double*. Wheaton: The Theosophical Publishing House.

———. 1927. *The Astral Body*. Wheaton: The Theosophical Publishing House.

Ramacharaka, Y. 1903. *Fourteen Lessons in Yogi Philosophy*. Chicago: The Yoga Publication Society.

———. 1904. *Advanced Course in Yogi Philosophy and Oriental Occultism*. Chicago: The Yoga Publication Society.

———. 1937. *The Life Beyond Death*. Chicago: The Yoga Publication Society.

Raudive, K. 1971. *Breakthrough: An Amazing Experiment in Electronic Communication with the Dead*. Gerrards Cross: Smythe.

Ring, J. 1980. *Life at Death*. New York: Coward-McCann.

———.1984. *Heading Toward Omega*. New York: Morrow.
Ritchie, G. G. 1978. *Return from Tomorrow*. Waco: Chosen Books.
Roberts, J. 1970. *The Seth Material*. Englewood Cliffs: Prentice-Hall.
———.1972. *Seth Speaks*. Englewood Cliffs: Prentice-Hall.
———.1974. *Nature of Personal Reality*. Englewood Cliffs: Prentice-Hall.
———.1975. *Adventures in Consciousness*. Englewood Cliffs: Prentice-Hall.
———.1979. *The Nature of the Psyche*. Englewood Cliffs: Prentice-Hall.
———.1986. *Seth: Dreams and Projection of Consciousness*. Walpole: N. H. Stillpoint.
Robinson, L.W. 1981. *Is It True What They Say About Edgar Cayce?* New York: Berkley.
Rogo, D.W. 1983. *Leaving the Body: A Complete Guide to Astral Projection*. Englewood Cliffs: Prentice-Hall.
Steiger, B. 1978. *You Will Live Again*. New York: Dell.
——— and L. Williams. 1976. *Other Lives*. New York: Award.
Stern, J. 1967. *Edgar Cayce: The Sleeping Prophet*. New York: Bantam.
Stevenson, I. 1966. *Twenty Cases Suggestive of Reincarnation*. New York: Amer. Soc. Psychic. Res.
Sugrue, T. 1942. *There Is a River*. [biography of Edgar Cayce] New York: Dell.
Sutphen, D. 1976. *You Are Born Again to Be Together*. New York: Simon & Schuster.
———.1978. *Past Lives, Future Loves*. New York: Simon & Schuster.
Swann, I. 1975. *To Kiss Earth Good-Bye*. New York: Hawthorne.
Tambiah, S. J. 1970. *Buddhism and the Spirit Cults of Northeast Thailand*. Cambridge: Cambridge University Press.
Tebecis, A.K., 1982. *Mahikari, Thank God for the Answers at Last*. Tokyo: L. H. Yoko Shuppan.
Verlag, A. 1977. *Secret Doctrines of the Tibetan Book of the Dead*. Boulder: Shambhala.
Wambaugh, H. 1978. *Reliving Past Lives*. New York: Bantam.
———.1979. *Life Before Life*. New York: Bantam.

Wedeck, H.E. 1971. *Dictionary of Spiritualism*. New York: Philosophical Library.
Wickland, C.A. 1974. *Thirty Years Among the Dead*. Hollywood: Newcastle.
Woodward, M.A. 1972. *Edgar Cayce's Story of Karma*. New York: Berkley.
Zaretsky, I. 1966. *Bibliography on Spirit Possession and Spirit Mediumship*. Berkeley: University of California Press.

* About the Author

Edith Fiore, Ph.D., graduated with a doctorate in clinical psychology from the University of Miami. She first became interested in hypnosis when she attended a workshop in self-hypnosis at the Esalen Institute, and she began to incorporate hypnosis into her therapy fourteen years ago. The author of YOU HAVE BEEN HERE BEFORE: A PSYCHOLOGIST LOOKS AT PAST LIVES, Dr. Fiore now practices psychology in Saratoga, California.